WHITE WOMEN CRY AND CALL ME ANGRY

WHITE WOMEN CRY AND CALL ME ANGRY

A BLACK WOMAN'S MEMOIR ON RACISM IN PHILANTHROPY

YANIQUE REDWOOD

WHITE WOMEN CRY AND CALL ME ANGRY:
A Black Woman's Memoir on Racism in Philanthropy

Copyright © 2023 by Yanique Redwood

All rights reserved. Except for brief quotations in critical articles and reviews, no part of this book may be reproduced in any manner without prior written permission from the author.

Cover Design: Safiy David Sanchez

eBook ISBN: 979-8-9886064-0-6
Paperback ISBN: 979-8-9886064-1-3

❀ Created with Vellum

To Black women who lead in their families, schools, neighborhoods, faith communities, and workplaces. I see you.

black women breathe flowers, too.
just because
we are taught to grow them in the lining of our quiet (our
grandmothers secret)
does not mean
we do not swelter with wild tenderness.
we soft swim.
we petal.
we scent limbs.
love.
we just have been too long a garden for sharp and deadly teeth.
so we
have
grown
ourselves
into
greenhouses.

—Nayyirah Waheed[1], *Salt*

---

1. I just love artists who gift us with their work while remaining anonymous. I was unable to get permission to publish this poem, but I hope Nayyirah Waheed will be supportive of my usage. This poem is deeply resonant.

CONTENTS

Author's Note	xi
Foreword	xiii
Introduction	xvii

PART I
ME

1. The Search	3
2. Tuskegee	9
3. Winners and Losers	13
4. The Dirty Truth	20

PART II
THEM

5. Not That Black	33
6. Sunshine and Pain	38
7. Token	46
8. A Letter to Freddie Gray	52
9. Unhinged	65
10. My Basement	94
11. A Pleasure Virgin Discovers the Antidote to Whiteness	99
12. Nicky	106

PART III
US

13. How Does It Feel to Be a Compromise?	129
14. Pulling Back the Curtain on Philanthropy	140
15. Tree of Life	148
16. Frequently Asked Questions	154
17. What Happened to Faith?	165
18. The Vote	176
Epilogue	186

Acknowledgments	203
References	207
About the Author	211

AUTHOR'S NOTE

This is a work of creative nonfiction that relies on my memory of events that took place over my life and career. Because memory can be hard to grasp at times, especially when attempting to reconstruct events for storytelling, I made every effort to verify details with others who were present to corroborate my story. In some cases, I have compressed or reordered conversations to better tell the story. I have occasionally changed names to protect the privacy of certain individuals. I acknowledge there are some who may not agree with my take on these events and may have evolved their perspectives since our interactions took place. I think everyone was doing their best to deal with a very challenging subject—racism. That said, I am sharing my opinions and interpretations from my social location as a Black woman at a particular point in time as I negotiated racism in the philanthropic sector. The opinions expressed in this collection are mine alone.

FOREWORD

Philanthropy has the power to facilitate transformational change in society. This power, fueled by the wealth of foundation endowments, is needed now more than ever as daily headlines of efforts to diminish democratic values and civil rights are commonplace. Thank goodness for the forward-thinking, progressive talent found in many foundations around the country that invest in equity and justice; their work shines a bright light on the promise of America.

I believe Black women are the most courageous leaders in philanthropy. This belief mirrors the well-documented contributions of Black women across a variety of sectors in the United States. Similar to historic and current day leaders like Sojourner Truth, Fannie Lou Hamer, Kamala Harris, and Stacy Abrams; philanthropy boasts a long list of Black sheroes. Throughout my years in philanthropy, I have had the pleasure of working with brilliant Black women who lead their foundations with intention and courage.

However, the unspoken truth – the difficult and painful reality – is that we pay grave consequences for leading in the philanthropic sector. Our stories have remained silent...until now.

I first met Dr. Yanique Redwood as I was leaving the Annie E. Casey Foundation after a nine-year tenure and she was arriving as a new employee. I was immediately blown away by her brilliance. I remember her being both "quiet and smart," and she had all the credentials needed to succeed there. I recall admiring Yanique from the start, while simultaneously worrying about how she would fare. I knew all too well what nondiverse, privileged foundations can do to a young Black professional—a young Black woman at that. I prayed that her obvious talent, and the weight of her credentials, would shield her from some of the experiences I had while on the "inside." As I left Casey, I knew that I would see her from time to time, as she was a "next-generation star" at the foundation.

Just two short years later, I received the wonderful news that Yanique was appointed president and CEO of the Consumer Health Foundation in Washington, DC. She had made it! Her transition to the foundation C-Suite was not surprising, given her talent, yet it was a very different experience from that of the majority of Black women in the sector who do not go on to become CEO. Yanique became active in the Association of Black Foundation Executives (ABFE), where I serve as president and CEO. She quickly became one of the leading foundation CEOs in Washington, DC, as well as the nation on the issues of racial equity and justice. I was thrilled at her success. Yet soon thereafter, she disappeared. Yanique stopped coming to field events and wasn't too responsive to my outreach about ABFE's work. That was not like her, and I didn't understand why. Her book helps me understand what happened.

White Women Cry and Call Me Angry: A Black Woman's Memoir on Racism in Philanthropy is a detailed account of how difficult it is for Black women to navigate the predominately white foundation sector in the United States. Her story unveils the complex dynamics involved when "leading while a Black woman" with an intentional focus on racial justice. Yanique talks about it all: how workplace racism inflicts self-doubt, her struggles with depression, and her experiences of humiliation.

Yet given these obstacles, this work is a story about how amazing Black women in philanthropy are. Yanique prevailed and excelled. She ascended to the top ranks of philanthropy (which can be a lonely place for Black women) and led the historic transformation of the Consumer Health Foundation into if, A Foundation for Radical Possibility. As a gift to the reader, she describes the pain, lessons, and healing she experienced throughout her journey.

Over my career, I have counseled hundreds of Black women in foundations around the country on the topics of effective leadership and career mobility. The same themes that Yanique writes about in her book ring true for many of us working in these predominately white spaces. This book provides firsthand perspective on what to expect when a Black woman's career is focused on transformation, equity, and change for all communities. While Yanique speaks about philanthropy, this book is a must-read for all women of color who find themselves navigating white-dominant culture and anti-Blackness in any workplace. White partners in philanthropy also need to read this book; I ask that you sit in your discomfort and be open to personal reflection and growth.

I am inspired when I read this work. Black women have changed the world, and we owe it to ourselves to speak our truth and to share our stories to continue this legacy. To my sisters, you will get tired and hit the wall. When you do, reread select essays in this book to recharge. I want to personally thank Yanique for her candor and honesty, and I know she does this out of her love for Black women. I will share this work with others, and I ask that you do the same. There is too much at stake to keep these stories inside because this world needs more Black women leaders everywhere.

Susan Taylor Batten
President and CEO
ABFE, A Philanthropic Partnership for Black Communities

INTRODUCTION

> There is no agony like bearing an
> untold story inside of you.
> —Zora Neale Hurston, *Dust Tracks on a Road*

The title *White Women Cry and Call Me Angry* is simply a container for all kinds of behaviors that white women engage in to maintain their positions of power when people of color assert themselves. The stories in this essay collection recount interactions between me and real-life white women. Real words were exchanged. Real heartbreak happened. If you are a Black woman or other woman of color who has survived (or is surviving) racial abuse in the workplace, you are the audience for this book. The setting just happens to be philanthropy, a sector where foundation staff give away money to nonprofit organizations, at least 5 percent of their endowments annually, as required by the IRS. In 2012, at the age of thirty-seven, I landed the job of president and CEO of a private foundation in the nation's capital called Consumer Health Foundation (referred to as CHF throughout the collection, though now rebranded as **if**, A Foundation for Radical Possibility). In my world, that's a big deal. Not many Black women, especially those as young as I was, reach this position.

I decided to write a book because my colleagues in the philanthropic sector from across the United States were asking how we did such incredible work with such a small endowment. At the time, our endowment was valued at approximately $25 million, small in comparison with the likes of the multi-billion-dollar endowment of the Robert Wood Johnson Foundation, also a health foundation. However, I wasn't interested in writing about the mechanics of our work, answering questions such as "Do you get market rate returns on your socially responsible investments?" While these mechanics are important, I wanted to tell the story of our foundation from different angles.

First, I wanted to tell the story of the foundation's transformation. It is a beautiful story, and I believe every foundation should know about it. To be clear, though, the transformation I describe did not happen without considerable friction. We had to confront our own biases and the ways in which we had internalized harmful norms that impeded our ability to do our bravest work.

Our transformation also happened in the wake of the Black Lives Matter movement and in the context of the election of Donald Trump, the storming of the Capitol, and the murders of so many Black people at the hands of police and vigilantes. This backdrop must be acknowledged and accounted for if you are to really understand the importance of the radical shifts in culture, practices, and programs that the foundation has undergone. We were aiming to model the very actions we were asking of local governments, nonprofits, and philanthropic partners at a time when everything was at stake.

Second, I wanted to convey my internal life as a leader and share some of the experiences that led me to the sector. I don't believe we can understand organizations and how they function if we don't also consider the back stories of the people leading and working in them. Third, I wanted to expose the racial dynamics happening behind the scenes in the do-good sector, which is no less susceptible to racism than any other sector in American[1] society. Foundations are conceived and birthed in the same rancid, racist waters that we all swim in. Trace the history of most any foundation endowment and you will find racism.

And when I became worn down by the racial abuse I encountered in the sector, I decided to record stories that could illuminate my struggle and telegraph to other Black women and women of color: you are not alone. Zora Neale Hurston reminds us, "There is no agony like bearing an untold story inside of you" (2006, 97). I no longer want to bear this story, and I hope no Black woman or other woman of color ever has to struggle in silence. For me, this book is not about shaming anyone. At one point in my journey, it was intended to be a call in. But it is no longer a call in or call out. It is about my ability to name what happened to me and to be in community with others who have had similar experiences. It is another step toward healing, though I am aware of the risks I take in doing so.

You should know that I debated centering white women in the title of this essay collection. I felt I was giving away my power by doing so. I also asked myself, What about white men? They, too, have inflicted their fair share of direct harm, even as they hover as silent and invisible progenitors of the socio-emotional harm I describe in these essays. Nevertheless, I decided to name white women because they dominate this sector, and their intersectional identities (for example, white and Jewish) led to dynamics that I believe need to be interrogated.

I also name white women because it was hand-to-hand combat with them between 2012 and 2018 that finally broke me. In the process of picking up the pieces from this combat, I awakened to an entirely new way of leading. I adopted the wisdom from a T-shirt, of all places: "I Am the Work." It reminded me of the oft-quoted "Be the Change You Wish to See." After years of trying to convert white women to my antiracism cause, I was exhausted. I needed to stop and look inside. So I set out to accomplish two goals: heal myself and transform my institution.

I started writing seriously in 2018 to process trauma, in both my personal life and my professional life, but when I began sharing drafts with a few early readers, one of them said she felt something was missing. "Where is your rage?" she asked. "You sound detached." When I looked back at what I had written, I couldn't deny her observation. On a radio show in 1961, author James Baldwin said, "To be a Negro in this country and to be relatively conscious is to be in a state of rage almost all of the time."

I did sometimes feel the rage Baldwin spoke of, but I was more often teary, speechless, paralyzed, numb (maybe even a bit dissociative), and dying inside. Instead of expressing outwardly, I often turned inward to cope, emotionally and socially distancing myself within the sector as often as I could. Responses to trauma can manifest in myriad ways. Some of us lash out, expressing justifiable rage. Some of us power up. Some of us shut down and withdraw altogether. Sometimes we do all the above. I hope we allow Black women and other women of color multiple ways to process and respond to this trauma. Racism is a lot.

This book is organized in three sections, with several essays within each section. At the end of each essay, I have provided some guiding questions to help you examine the themes emerging from the essay before moving on to the next essay. In section I, I share stories from my early years as a child experiencing parental abuse while coming to grips with social hierarchies based on race, skin color, class, gender, and nationality. I also share stories of me as a young woman radicalized in college, graduate school, and while working in a community where Black people were acutely experiencing poverty. By "radicalized," I mean learning to grasp things at the root, per Angela Davis. I hope these stories will help you understand my convictions and why I took the posture that I did in the sector and in my foundation.

In section II, I turn to essays that describe the experiences with white women that prompted the title of this essay collection. These were some of the toughest essays to write. I wrote about these encounters in detail and included receipts (i.e., email exchanges) whenever I could. With this level of sometimes exacting detail, I was afraid I might lose you, the reader. But it felt important to convey how racism shows up—in the minutiae and subterfuge that often constitute our day-to-day interactions.

It's also important to say that many of these interactions took place in spaces that the Washington Regional Association of Grantmakers (WRAG) curated. WRAG is the hub for philanthropic collaboration in DC. But I do not hold WRAG's former or current leadership responsible for my experiences of harm. The former leader Tamara Copeland nurtured me. Ruth LaToison Ifill is the Black woman who is currently leading WRAG. She needs our support.

Section III consists of stories about my foundation's decolonization, which author Edgar Villanueva defines as the process of stopping the cycles of abuse and healing ourselves from trauma. He says in *Decolonizing Wealth: Indigenous Wisdom to Heal Divides and Restore Balance*, "We must identify and reject the colonized aspects of our culture and institutions so that we can heal. ... Instead of *divide, control, exploit*, we embrace a paradigm of *connect, relate, belong*" (2018, 34). When I could no longer take the racial abuse in the broader sector, I turned inward to confront the tensions and racist behaviors within our own progressive institution. And we rose to the challenge. There is light toward the end of this book, and the foundation's two new co-leaders, Temi F. Bennett and Hanh Le, are continuing to lead the way.

As you engage with the stories in this essay collection, I hope you will take away an understanding of the deep and abiding impact of racism on the body and mind. As a consequence of the interactions that I describe in these essays, I am afraid of what racism-related stress has done to both my physical and mental health. By grace and conviction (and the privilege of assets), I have been healing while on an island in the Caribbean, and I am grateful for the spaciousness to do so. I wish this for all of us—extended time away from the brutality of racism in the U.S. context and the ways in which it wears you down (more to come on "weathering," a term coined by my graduate school professor Arline Geronimus to convey the detrimental impact of racism-related stress on the body).

Part of my healing process also includes writing this book. I share these hard stories because they can no longer live inside of me. I must tell these stories and find those with similar stories so we can bear witness to each other. I must also tell the stories I couldn't protect my Black young adult daughter from having *inside of* her to tell.

In her first workplace experience after graduate school, a white woman in a leadership role told my 25-year-old daughter (who had been an advocate for antiracism in the work of this organization) that because she is from a Black middle-class family, she can afford a lifestyle (pointing to a yacht docked outside of their conference hotel) that this supervisor could not because she grew up poor. This same white woman had been resisting work on antiracism. Thankfully, a Black woman, Maegan Scott, created a consulting firm where these kinds of microaggressions don't exist and thus do not have to be negotiated. My daughter got a job there and is now thriving. She is lucky. So many of us are not.

Throughout this collection, you will notice many mentions of my heart beating inside my chest. I am using this platform to name for myself and others the circumstances with white people and within institutionalized white supremacy that made my heart beat fast and hard. Doctors call these heart palpitations, and they are often attributed to stress, anxiety, and panic attacks, which can ultimately contribute to the body's weathering. I want to make it clear that racism matters for health, mental health, maternal health, and longevity.

In addition, I used the visceral and embodied memories of my heart beating inside my chest to signal that a story was worth telling. While I started writing about my professional trauma for my own healing, I now know that I write for all of us who do the work of racial and social justice even though our hearts race, thump, break, and shatter into little pieces like shards of glass, only to find a way to reassemble, heal, and believe again. I tell these stories for all of us leading change, wherever we find ourselves.

---

1. In this work, I use the term "America" interchangeably with the United States of America. America also means the countries that make up North and South America, but here I am referring to the U.S.A.

PART I

ME

1

THE SEARCH

The trauma said, 'Don't write these poems. Nobody wants to hear you cry about the grief inside your bones.'
—Andrea Gibson, *The Madness Vase*

I AM CALLING OFF THE SEARCH FOR MY CHILDHOOD SELF. SHE WENT missing thirty-some years ago, but I have continued looking for her on the off chance she might still be out there trying to find her way back to me. The last time I saw her, she was about ten years old. When she wasn't wearing her starched navy-blue school uniform, she wore light cotton rompers and sturdy sandals, footwear good for all-day romping. Her mom was a stickler for clean, well-groomed children. Her hair was often neatly plaited in sections, with a large bow lodged on top, and her arms and legs shiny with baby oil.

Despite her family's middle-class Jamaican sensibilities, she was a bit of a bumptious child. When she was a toddler and didn't get her way, she repeatedly hit her forehead on any available wall until someone responded. She spoke her mind, always. "Uncle Basil, your shoes don't match your pants," she once said, and the adults hesitated and then roared with laughter. When she wasn't engaging the adults, she roamed the gated yard, sometimes wearing her mom's platform heels and pretending to be much older than her age.

She picked cherries right from the overgrown tree that guarded the gated driveway, its branches reaching down toward her with both ripe and ripening fruit. She grinned each time she tasted the juicy insides before spitting out the odd-shaped seed. She stooped low to inhale the fragrance from the peppermint plants that grew along the driveway, the leaves tickled by the fuzzy black caterpillars that crawled along their undersides. She patrolled the pomegranate, ackee, and papaya trees—none of them native to Jamaica but central to life on the island nonetheless—anxiously awaiting their annual production, as though a conductor somewhere gave the cue.

While the yard was hers to explore, the street was the real playground. Her neighborhood best friend, Lisa, and brother Shane lived opposite her house and adjacent to the gully at the street's dead end. When private telephone lines came to the neighborhood, she called Lisa up and waved out the window and asked, "Can you see me?" Across from them, brothers Richard and Oliver lived with their chatty mother, who monopolized the telephone line, which in those days was shared by two households. Sisters Julie and Jackie lived next door. A troupe of kids lived toward the other end, but this was her real crew. She and her younger sister played hopscotch, Simon Says, jump rope, and marbles in the street with friends while the adults watched from behind grilled verandas, slatted windows, and stoppered front doors.

One weekend afternoon, her dad strung a net across the street and tied the ends to two electric poles, and everyone—children and adults—played badminton for hours. Each time a car approached, her dad lifted the net and let the car through, and in no time the game was on again. That night on the front lawn of their house, her mom's fingers wove between hers and her sister's. Their friends completed the circle by doing the same as they sang "Ring around the Rosie." "Ashes, ashes, we all fall down!" she cried with glee as she plunged onto the welcoming grass, her heart full of love and connection.

There were street parties on some nights just for the adults, and she fell asleep to the pulsating rhythms of reggae interspersed with laughter, confident that tomorrow would bring new adventures, even if they were not always the fun kind. Like the time her dad taught her a lesson after she'd used a red marker to color in the white number seven sealed into the concrete column at the front gate. The next day, the sun rose high in the sky and began to set again before the number seven, with help from bleach, soapy water, a scrub brush, and her preadolescent fingers, turned from red to pink to white again. Or there was the time she threw a rock and hit Jackie in the forehead. Oh, she got a beating for that!

* * *

I MOVED to the United States as I was turning ten. My parents rented one half of a duplex in a working-class Black neighborhood in Lauderhill, Florida. It was a step down for sure, though we still had a yard and neighbors, and kids still played in the streets. Two years later, I got into painting T-shirts and braiding colorful box-stitch keychains using flat plastic yarn. It turns out that I could make pretty good pocket money selling junk. My sister had an inclination for taking my things without permission, and I was positive that she was responsible when I discovered a T-shirt missing one day.

Not one for extending the benefit of the doubt, not now and not then, I confronted her. She denied it. We argued as I chased her around the room, hopping on and off the twin beds, but she would not admit to taking the T-shirt. I am not sure when or if I decided it would be a good idea to choke my sister, but that is exactly what I was doing when my dad stormed into our bedroom demanding to know what was going on. "She stole my T-shirt!" I exclaimed.

I was resolute: I was right, and my sister was wrong. Thus I was stunned when he left the room, returned with his broad leather belt, and settled into beating me, right there in the hallway outside the bedroom, adjacent to the bathroom where my mom was taking a shower. I had gotten spankings before, but this one felt unlike any other. From this beating, I needed protection, but no one came to rescue me.

Later that evening, I sat in the family room at the back of the flat, alone and in the dark, feeling numb and dazed, my skin still tingling from the lashes. My father, who had been my hero up until that day, stepped into the darkness, sat down next to me, and said, "Daddy didn't mean to hurt you." His words confused me. He had never apologized for spankings, and why did he use "Daddy" instead of "I"? I don't remember my mom saying anything to me or him. She said she did but behind closed doors.

For a long time, I wasn't the same. I slept some nights with a knife under my pillow, and on and off into my twenties, I kept one close by in my nightstand or on the floor under the bed. The knife is now gone, but the threat of danger is not. I feel it lurking and try to anticipate how and when it might nab me so that I can take more care. Sadness, too, hangs out close by, waiting for just the right moment to move in. I use journaling, talk therapy, sometimes Lexapro to forestall them both. One of my Black woman therapists surmised that my dad had probably struggled during the Reagan years, when trickle-down economics was all the rage and tax cuts for the wealthy did nothing for Black working-class people's economic prospects. "Not an excuse," she said; "just context." For this and other reasons, I eventually forgave him. But I suppose I am still not the same.

In my journal, I look for her—my childhood self, the one who giggled and frolicked, the one who happily greeted each day, the one who sought out friends and felt safe and unhindered. I join social clubs in hopes of finding her, but it just ends up being me, feeling timid and awkward. I start hobbies and projects to reconnect with her, like the vegetable garden that lasted only one growing season. Maybe she failed to show because I didn't plant any cherries or mint. I stare at pictures of her in old photo albums and smile. I love her and forgive her for staying away. It's easy to be kind to her.

In my journal, I question who I would have become had it not been for that beating. There were others before and since, but that one left a mark. Maybe I was just sensitive at the onset of menses, or maybe my father's frustration with his economic condition found its way that day into his belt. An entry in my first diary, a small chunky thing with purple and white flowers, hearts, and sunbursts, hints at the latter. On June 9, 1988, I wrote, Daddy lost his job Friday and Monday he hit me very hard. Either way, without that beating, I wonder if I would have married the man who made me laugh and then made me cry, the one who pushed me into a ditch on the side of a Toronto highway, the one who killed himself on a beautiful fall morning.

I think about whether I would have taken another path in life, instead of being pulled toward the searing pain of racial injustice and its own relentless soul beatings. I try to imagine different trajectories, different stories unfolding, but none of them have a middle, much less an ending. These altered stories lead nowhere until they disappear, poof—just like she did. I'm tired now, so I am ending the search. There is no assurance that she is coming back. I recently planted a cherry tree to honor the memory that we were once innocent and carefree.

Guiding Questions:

- What is the grief, from the distant or recent past, that lives in your bones?
- How does this grief influence the work you do today?

2

TUSKEGEE

The wound is the place where the Light enters you.
—Rumi

BA BUMP. BA BUMP. I FEEL MY HEART BEAT. BA BUMP. BA BUMP. BA *bump.* It beats harder. Faster. I fight tears, but they march forward. They tell me they will not go back. A hole in my chest widens and deepens. I pant. I look to my right. There is a bank of windows along the outer wall. It is sunny outside. Maybe if someone opens just one window, I will feel less like I am falling down, down, down a dark hole. I turn to my left. Though I am sitting in the second row in a small classroom, the door, my only exit, feels far away.

I am taking an elective, one I thought would be a throwaway. There are only a few more classes between me and my bachelor of science in chemistry. The elective is Sociology of Medicine, and Dr. Sokolovsky stands at the podium. In painstaking detail, she recounts the forty-year history of the US Public Health Service study of untreated syphilis in 600 poor Black men (399 of them with active syphilis disease) in Tuskegee, Alabama. Some passed the disease on to their wives and therefore to their unborn children. Others died even when penicillin afforded white men a cure, a chance to hide their secrets, a chance to live. I am not an American southerner. I am a Black immigrant, and I am only twenty-one. I am a woman, but this feels personal. Surreal. My head spins. How can humans do this to other humans? I have to get out of here.

I find Dr. Sokolovsky's office and wait for her. I pace the hallway. I sit on the dull tiled floor with my back leaning against her large wooden door. My chest still caves. She shows up. I am snot-faced. It isn't pretty. She invites me in to sit down. She is a short, plump woman with creamy pale skin and a mop of curly strawberry blonde hair. She tilts her head in her usual way, at an almost forty-five-degree angle, while listening. I plead with her to explain. "How could this be?" She eventually tells me that I can funnel my anger and frustration. She says something about a public health degree. I am bleary-eyed and have never heard of such a thing, but I am relieved that I can do something with this pain coursing through me.

For the remainder of the semester, I see what was previously unseen. My professors, they are largely white. The cafeteria workers are Black. So are the women cleaning the dormitory bathrooms, stinking with pools of vomit from white girls' hangovers. I smile harder now at the workers. I want them to know that I see them, though I lower my eyes as I walk away, ashamed of what I am discovering about their own life chances and mine.

I frantically reorder my life. I finish my chemistry degree, though I will never swirl a beaker or read a periodic table again. I network and land an internship in an agency that is a sister to the agency responsible for the syphilis study. Under my mentor Dr. Rueben Warren, I study the impacts of exposure to lead-based paint on the intellectual and behavioral development of Black boys. We hypothesize that boys who have been lead-poisoned act out in school. They have a hard time learning and are frustrated. Soon they are pipelined to juvie and then jails and prison. I take the GRE and apply to doctoral programs in public health. I will find a cure for what ails us. In my desperation I fail to see that I, too, must heal.

* * *

TEN YEARS LATER, I finish my dissertation and start a postdoctoral program at the Centers for Disease Control and Prevention (CDC) that combines epidemiology training with a two-year stint in the US Public Health Service. Just like everyone else in the large conference room on orientation day, I am wearing a khaki-colored uniform, consisting of a collared shapeless shirt tucked into equally shapeless trousers, except mine has been secretly stitched in violation of the regulations to provide just a bit of shaping at the waist and hips. I wear my hair in locs, also against regulations, and pull them extra tight and pin them down, hoping to hide them from my superiors. I am among scores of new Commissioned Corps officers stationed at CDC for two years, to be deployed all over the planet to fight mostly infectious diseases.

When the speaker finishes his presentation on the history of the US Public Health Service and fields questions from the other officers, I raise my hand from the rear left corner of the packed conference room. My comment is simple, but it holds so much for me. I can feel my heart beating again in my chest. *Ba bump. Ba bump.* I breathe in and then out to calm myself. I have to say something. He calls on me. "You didn't mention the Syphilis Study at Tuskegee led by the US Public Health Service." The room is silent. I feel a heaviness descend. He fumbles to respond. My mind goes blank. I can't tell you what he said.

. . .

GUIDING QUESTIONS:

- When did you first come to understand the institutional and structural nature of racism?
- How did it feel to speak out about it? If you chose to stay quiet, why did you make that choice?

3

WINNERS AND LOSERS

> There are still winners and losers, the powerful and the powerless, and the claim that everyone is in it together is an eraser of the inconvenient realities of others.
> —Anand Giridharadas, *Winners Take All*

THERE IS A SCAR ON MY RIGHT KNEE, SLIGHTLY BIGGER THAN A quarter. The skin is translucent in the spot that got skinned back in Jamaica when I was in second or third grade. I remember it as if it were yesterday. One of the girls in our Catholic primary school brought a pale-skinned doll to campus. Imagine ten or so girls in starched navy-blue romper dresses over white collared shirts swarming the girl with the doll, everyone trying to touch it or at least get a peek. Imagine us all falling to the ground after a push from behind sent us tumbling and getting bruised in the process. Imagine some of us lining up at the nurse's office to get our cuts cleaned with Dettol, followed by the application of mercurochrome, and whimpering from the sting as we walked back to class. At that age, I didn't have the word for white, but that doll was something to be coveted. The girls in my school who had light brown skin and long wavy hair also seemed more special in some way. More special than me.

My mom delivered me, her firstborn, at University Hospital in Kingston, Jamaica, in 1975. My sister followed in 1978. Two years later, the bloodiest election in Jamaica's history claimed more than eight hundred lives, and my parents made a commitment then to get out amid political unrest and food shortages. My dad's mother had migrated to the United States years earlier and filed for us. We left the island in 1985 with the privilege of our papers. Before we left, I had already formed early ideas about winners and losers and the role skin color and class played in determining who would be a winner and who would be a loser. But at such a young age, I had no words for what I was feeling. Yet the famous doll study led by Black psychologists Kenneth and Mamie Clark in the 1940s and subsequent re-creations of the study have taught us that children don't need words like *race* and *racism*. Very early on in their development, children as young as five, both Black and white, believe that Black equals ugly and bad and white equals pretty and nice, even though nothing could be further from the truth.

Before migrating to the States from Jamaica, I did not know I was Black. I did know, however, that my skin was somewhere between fair and dark. I was also in the middle in other respects. My parents drove a Triumph Dolomite, a British car they bought used and yellow and painted a ruddy brown color. Some of my classmates arrived in nicer white or silver cars, probably Hondas from Japan. The two boys with the darkest skin—both always in trouble and severely beaten by the teachers—walked into the schoolyard each morning, their shoes begging bread. Even though I did not yet know I was Black nor that most of us were Black, I had already intuited something about complexion, class, and treatment. I used to sit on the stone wall across from the classroom buildings and watch my wealthier schoolmates play. I did not belong to that crowd. My primary school friend, Tammy, later told me she had gone to a schoolmate's birthday party and remembered being in awe of the sheer size of the house lodged in the hills above the capital city of Kingston. She also remembered the poor kids lining up under the tree outside at lunch to get a traditional Jamaican snack of bun and cheese and milk, while the rest of us sat inside the cafeteria and ate what our parents had packed for us.

The morning we left for America, it was still dark outside. I felt my mother's gentle rustle and heeded her whispered instructions to get dressed. In the days leading up to our departure, I neither asked my mom and dad, "What about my friends?" as a typical ten-year-old might nor considered my aunts and uncles who were staying behind. My godmother, who had moved to New Jersey years before, used to ship gifts to us from America—foods, soaps, and other sundries that were hard to find or just not available. What I enjoyed most was Kellogg's Corn Flakes, the plain kind in the box with the giant red, green, and yellow rooster. How I loved getting corn flakes from America. It was a nice change of pace from creamy cornmeal porridge, which I did love with its nutmeg, cinnamon, and condensed milk cooked in. But this was even better. It came from America! Whenever the barrel arrived with my godmother's goodies, I imagined America must be magical. What manner of place could produce such treats? I yearned to find out.

My life in Jamaica and my life in the United States paralleled each other in many ways. The sun shone almost every day in South Florida. The houses and duplexes were like those on my island street—concrete low rises with a little patch of grass out front. No one in my new neighborhood had a gate or fruit trees, however. Every house on my street back home had gates fashioned out of iron and at least an ackee, papaya, or naseberry tree.

A confusing series of events in America started to shape my

eventual interest in marginalization and oppression. The first and most puzzling moment unfolded in the schoolyard of Royal Palm Elementary School. Because we behaved and excelled in school, a few peers and I were given the status of patrol officer. Across our chests we wore neon orange belts, which attached to belts that snapped in place around our waists. We monitored the schoolyard with teachers, both in the mornings and at the end of the school day, and advised adults of any problems requiring their attention.

I was in the fifth grade, so I was eleven or so, when a younger Black boy walked right up to me with tears welling in his eyes and eventually rolling down his face. He turned and pointed an accusatory finger at another boy, also Black, and said, "He called me a Jamaican." I had heard kids tease others about being Haitian, but Jamaican? I am Jamaican! There is nothing wrong with me! I turned this incident over and over in my head after school that day and the days that followed. I couldn't understand how it got decided that some people were bad simply based on where they came from and then were teased because of it.

At the same time, my father, who struggled to find work as an accountant, drove me to school in an embarrassing taxicab with the Marlboro Man sitting confidently atop. He also delivered pizza for Domino's in our family's gray Chevy Celebrity, and in the wee hours of the morning, he tossed newspapers from the window of our car onto manicured lawns before the sprinklers turned on for the sod's morning shower. My mother, on the other hand, worked in an office. She made $3 per hour answering phones in a tiny room in a tiny office in a tiny building about twenty minutes away from home, where she sat at a round table all day next to others who smoked cigarettes and answered phones. Her job as a supervisor at the government-run telephone company in Jamaica probably got her this job in an office, but unlike her government job, this one offered nothing—no health insurance, no housing allowance, no transportation allowance, and definitely no pension. It didn't feel as though we were in the middle anymore. It felt as though we were on the bottom.

I was also navigating tensions at home. I never saw my father hit my mother, but patriarchy—again, I had no words for it at the time—showed up in our family. For example, when my dad got a stable nine-to-five job, we couldn't eat dinner until he came home from work. If he was late, my mom would allow my sister and me to eat, but she would not do so until he sat down. When I was about fourteen or so, my father and I faced off when I intervened to defend my mom because I just couldn't take it anymore.

We had moved into a townhouse in the same general neighborhood as the duplex we first lived in when we arrived in the United States. My parents purchased it at an auction for $30,000 after two years of hustling. It became an asset and, along with the equity in the house in Jamaica, provided some cushion. They had brought with them a privilege that allowed them to surpass generations of poor Black people in this country who couldn't dream of ever buying a home. It irritates me when people compare Black middle-class immigrants' "successes" with the "failures" of slave-descended poor Black people in America. This is not an apples-to-apples comparison. If you got on a plane to get to the States, you brought some privileges on that flight with you.

The townhouse was a disaster when my parents bought it. A hideous blue-and-cream paisley print covered the kitchen walls, and bright red paint coated the walls in the bedroom that would become mine. Graffiti, holes, and smashed bathroom mirrors screamed eviction. But little by little, my parents fixed it up. They laid down large, white tiles on the first floor and ran a vibrant peach-colored carpet all the way up the staircase steps to the upstairs bedrooms. Over a series of Saturdays, my mom, my sister, and I sponged down the kitchen walls with water (as my new baby sister looked on) to aid in peeling the wallpaper, and my dad converted the garage into a den that my mom later used to run a daycare when she could no longer take working for others.

My mom loved her spacious new bedroom. Light streamed in from the glass sliding door to fill it, and the bathroom had a soaking tub separate from the shower. Isn't that the dream? My sister and I no longer shared a bathroom with our parents; we had one all to ourselves. It was from my room that I heard my father one day when he picked up the phone in his bedroom.

"Jez, it's time to come off di phone," he ordered.

Embarrassed for my mom, I jumped off my bed, marched down the hallway, and scolded, "You can't tell her what to do."

He stared at me. I stared back at him.

"Who yuh talking to?" his voice both threatening and disbelieving.

He didn't beat me that time, but I knew I had crossed the line. In a traditional Jamaican family, the man of the house reigned, and children were to be seen and not heard. But I just couldn't help it, and I didn't care. After years of him dictating what everyone in the house could and could not do, I had had enough. My mother would later implore, "Yanique, for a peaceful life, just don't say anything." I never listened to my mother, and I continued to pay for it.

This was the context in which I grew up. I was barely fourteen when these observations were imprinted. I couldn't get the pale-skinned doll out of my mind nor the way skin color and class separated my schoolmates and determined their treatment. I couldn't forget the kid with the tears who had been teased and called a Jamaican. I felt bad for the Haitians who would say they were from the Bahamas to escape bullying. I never could or would tolerate a man, like my father, telling a woman, like my mother, what to do. These memories gnawed at me over the years. They would not leave me alone. These early experiences had exposed me to social hierarchies. And I hated them. I hated them in Jamaica, and I especially hated them in America. I hated the fact that there were winners and losers.

Guiding Questions:

- What social hierarchies were you exposed to as a child?
- How did you feel when you were at the top of the hierarchy? How about when you were at the bottom?

4

THE DIRTY TRUTH

Trusting the people is the indispensable precondition for
revolutionary change.
—Paolo Freire, *Pedagogy of the Oppressed*

If you let my husband Ronnie tell the story of how we met, it will be different every time. Sometimes he will say that I sent him a drink from across a crowded room at a bar. Another time he will tell you that I walked up to him, also at a bar, and said, "Hey, shawty." But the reality was much less interesting. I had been working at Georgia State University when we met. This was a little more than a year after quitting my PhD program at University of Michigan ABD (all but dissertation). I left disillusioned by the academic enterprise and its prioritization of research and writing and the consumption of both by other people with PhDs. No Black person struggling to get by would ever read a paper I wrote. Not ever.

During one class discussion, I inquired about the possibility that the university might transfer control of a research center partnership (one that had been formed between the university and residents of Detroit to address community concerns) to the community. The professor admitted that the university would lose the indirect cost income that it received from grants to support the partnership. At the time, universities charged upward of 50 percent of grant dollars for indirect costs such as office equipment, supplies, administration, and the like. Ohh, I thought, the realization dawning on me. This was more about the money than transferring power to residents. I walked out of her classroom that day, knowing I would not return after the end of the semester. I could not live with the contradiction.

I left Michigan soon after with a master of public health that I had earned along the way to the PhD. I moved back home to Atlanta and got a job as a project manager for Georgia State University's newly launched public health program. My boss, Dr. Marshall Kreuter, a renowned health promotion expert, had come across a National Center for Minority Health and Health Disparities grant announcement to support community-based participatory research (CBPR), a form of research in which communities and researchers work in lockstep to identify neighborhood-based challenges, design solutions, and monitor outcomes. I had trained under CBPR researchers at Michigan, so I was thrilled to lend my expertise, particularly in a methodology called Photovoice, which involved giving cameras to people to document their health and lived realities from their own perspectives, helping them analyze those photos to identify root causes of issues, and then connecting them to policymakers to tell their stories to guide public policy.

The way the story goes, when my professor and closest mentor at Michigan, Dr. Caroline Wang, first developed and used Photovoice in Yunnan, China, with women rice farmers, she wanted to help guide the women in taking vivid photos. One of the women in the project took a photograph of another farmer in a rice field, but the subject was barely a dot amid a sea of green. On seeing the developed photo, Caroline advised the farmer to get closer to the subject next time. In response, the rice farmer said something like, "No, I wanted to show that this one woman has to farm this entire field of rice." Ahhh, herein lies the beauty of the Photovoice methodology. Only someone with lived experience of farming large paddies of rice could take *that* picture and tell *that* story of the hardship of women's labor. Professional, and even amateur, photographers may have expertise in taking beautiful, compelling shots, but they don't have the lived experience to tell a community's story of what is and is not important.

Before applying for the grant, we needed to meet with a community to determine if it wanted a relationship with the university, a risky proposition for communities that had been studied at length with few tangible results to show for it. Ideally, we would have been in an established relationship with a community, but that wasn't yet the case. Marshall made some initial inroads in one of twenty-five neighborhood planning units (NPUs) in Atlanta, NPU-V (V as in Victor). NPUs are citizen advisory councils that provide input to the mayor and city council on zoning, land use, and planning decisions. At the time, NPU-V was 92 percent Black, and most of its children lived in poverty. A mammoth baseball stadium, erected for the 1996 Olympics, stood on one end and brought white suburbanites into the city every spring to watch the Atlanta Braves play while scores of Black people making minimum wage served them popcorn and hot dogs.

On the south end of NPU-V, abutting Interstate 75/85, lay about thirty-four acres of industrial land that had been sitting vacant for decades. In the 1950s and 1960s, the Georgia State Highway Department ran the interstate highway through NPU-V, aligning with a federal effort that also impacted other Black communities across the country. The highway brought little benefit to the community and lots of detriments. Studies have shown that highways bring asthma-inducing pollution, and everyone I knew in NPU-V said the highway disrupted community cohesion. Against this backdrop, Marshall and I went to an evening meeting to talk with NPU-V's leadership about our idea for a codesigned research and action project on health in the five neighborhoods that make up NPU-V. Ronnie was there in his role as NPU-V's vice chair.

No matter what Ronnie tells you, this is how we really met—sitting across a table in a community meeting, me sitting upright in my dark suit, wearing glasses, and carrying a leather portfolio to take notes, and him slouching in his chair with long legs extended, wearing an unbuttoned shirt and a tie that hung loosely around his neck. He was handsome and charming, but his body language gave me pause. He will tell you he was tired from a long day at work. I read him as arrogant.

Marshall and I made our pitch, and after some back and forth, the community agreed to partner with us. But the chair of NPU-V, a strong-willed older Black woman named Ms. Peggy, who was rail thin and sickly because she had chronic obstructive pulmonary disease, had many rules. Rule #1: the community was going to lead. That was fine by us. We were there to share resources and power.

Together with NPU-V leadership and other residents, we planned to implement Caroline Wang's Photovoice approach and host forums to hear from community members about their health challenges. We also planned to use geographic information system (GIS) mapping to pinpoint rates of the top killers—cancer, diabetes, and heart disease. We designed a series of participatory processes to engage community members in selecting a disease to work on together, weighing both empirical data and qualitative data from community members' lived experience. I also decided at around the same time to finish my PhD. Caroline, who still mentored me from afar, said I didn't have to use the degree in narrowly defined ways—just to conduct research and write peer-reviewed journal articles. So, I negotiated with my dissertation committee to focus my research on the NPU-V Photovoice project.

The National Center for Minority Health and Health Disparities at NIH funded just a few CBPR projects. Ours was one of them. We received $1 million to spend over three years. As the project's director, my first task was to hire a project coordinator from the local community and attend a full-body NPU-V meeting to introduce myself. I walked into a packed room the night of the meeting and took my seat toward the back. It seemed that each agenda item caused some grumbling, whether it was a developer's pitch for zoning exceptions or a detail related to something like the NPU-V reunion cookout. Then it was my turn to speak. I assured myself that this would be short. I just needed to walk to the front of the room, say a little about myself and a little about Georgia State's interest in working with the community to address health issues, and introduce Susan[1], a well-connected mild-mannered older Black woman from the community, as the new project coordinator.

Before I could finish, Belinda, who had also applied to be project coordinator but had not been selected, screamed and walked out the side door of the community room. She came back in yelling about everything from lack of jobs to outsiders always coming into the community. The new NPU-V chair, Gloria, tried to get the meeting back under control, but nothing worked. All I could do was take my seat. As the program went on, I got up to find Ronnie. We had become friendly. He had expressed interest in learning more about Photovoice because of his work with community members on a photo activism project called the Dirty Dozen. We had met over lunch to compare notes. What I had initially perceived as arrogance was actually confidence and assuredness that came from feeling safe in the world, something that always felt just beyond my reach.

"What happened?" I asked, bewildered by what I had just

experienced. Unfazed, he replied, "This is how community meetings go sometimes." As a community organizer, he was familiar with the rage born of histories of extraction, loss, and pain. Belinda, a grandmother taking care of grandchildren, could not find work and was severely housing unstable. That job at the university with health benefits would have meant everything.

Shaken but steadfast, I launched Photovoice with two groups of people—established leaders in NPU-V and residents of McDaniel Glenn public housing who were disconnected from formal NPU processes—with the goal of better understanding each of their experiences of health in the neighborhood. Ronnie partnered with me on the project and served as our community organizer. I joined him as he knocked on doors in the public housing community and talked to people who were socially connected to each other but so isolated from the world I moved in. Watching his ease with people, the way he loved Black people and the way they loved him back, endeared me to him.

After weeks of recruiting, we hosted Photovoice interest meetings and prayed that people would show up. In the group of public housing residents, mostly women with children, people came but they were barely making it. Community meetings like these don't have a reputation of directly benefiting participants, so we offered a hot meal and a $50 stipend to make it somewhat worth their time. Folks shuffled in. Some were drunk but not loud drunk. This was the quiet, drooped eyelids, deeply depressed kind of drunk. It was hard to get them engaged in that first meeting.

We provided each person with a disposable camera. The assignment: use your camera to document the answer to the question, What does health mean to you? In about a week, we collected those cameras, and a week after that, we met again to review the developed pictures. Each person then selected two photos and spent time answering questions to deepen their root-cause analysis. The Photovoice methodology outlines these five questions:

What do you **S**ee here?
What is really **H**appening here?
How does this relate to **O**ur lives?
Why does this problem or strength exist?
What can we **D**o about it?

In the group of established NPU leaders, one of the young adults, Javon, sent his picture around the room: clothes, toys, and furniture were strewn on the sidewalk.

"What's your photograph called?" I asked him.

"It's called 'Trash.'"

"What do you see here?"

"I see trash."

"What is really happening here."

"People in this neighborhood are nasty. We keep our neighborhood trashy, and we have no pride."

Ronnie and I glanced at each other. I asked the next question.

"How does this relate to our lives?"

"We have to see this trash every day," he said as he rolled his eyes. "Don't nobody want to see this trash every day."

"Why does this problem exist?"

"It exists because we don't give a fuck about our community."

"What can we do about it?"

"We can stop throwing trash in the streets and come together to clean up our community."

I was gutted by the self- and community-directed hatred he was displaying, but as a researcher, my job was to allow his root-cause analysis to develop over time.

Ronnie, ever the organizer, took a different approach.

He asked Javon to look again. "What do you actually see in that picture?"

Javon slowed down and responded, "Clothes, toys, and furniture."

"Take another closer look. What is *really* happening here?"

Javon peered at the photograph, his eyes widening, the moment of discovery unfolding on his face. "This is an eviction."

Ronnie continued. "Why does this exist?

"Someone probably lost a job and couldn't afford to pay the rent." He added that this scene was playing out all over the neighborhood.

Others chimed in to share their sightings of people's belongings on front lawns and sidewalks. Eviction plagued this community.

Every time I recall this moment, it brings fresh tears to my eyes because of how we, myself included, have been duped into believing the worst about our communities.

After the first round of picture taking, more residents opened up. Cinnamon, a twenty-something mother of two in the group of public housing residents, presented a picture of two tiny bright spots surrounded by a grainy mix of black and brown darkness. The picture had been taken outside at night with very low lighting.

"What do you see here?" she asked, repeating the first SHOWeD question. "You can see one rat, but there were really two more there, you just can't see them. They all scattered." She said rats had invaded her apartment. The whole housing complex was infested. "I am trying to cook and rats are running across my stovetop and kitchen counter!" She looked as if she were in the moment of battle with the critters. She chronicled her desperate attempts to get the Atlanta Housing Authority to respond, including a petition she had created and got her neighbors to sign, but no one came to help. Everyone in the room backed her story.

There were many stories like this in both groups—stories of self-organized efforts, people calling the numbers provided to them by those in power, but those numbers led nowhere. It's why I titled my dissertation "The Numbers Don't Work for Us." This had been going on for years on end with no relief in sight. I had to muster everything I had to keep from crying in the middle of the sessions. I saw myself as a researcher and felt that I needed to be neutral and composed. But the stories were agonizing. I had never been at war with rats. The stories in both groups were hard. The stories in the group of public housing residents were harder.

After weeks of repeated photo taking and root-cause analysis, Ronnie and I worked with both groups to identify themes. Collectively, the stories revealed histories of white flight and abandonment, widespread levels of vacancy, deep and systemic government and private sector disinvestment, rampant speculative development, gentrification, and displacement. We also launched calling campaigns to flood the code enforcement office with requests for service, which led to some temporary relief, such as the boarding up of distressed vacant properties. At the larger community forum to select a disease to work on together, residents looked at all the empirical data on the top killers—heart disease, stroke, and cancer—and selected mental health. They said they felt deeply depressed and anxious. Many admitted to feelings of hopelessness, and some admitted to thoughts of suicide.

In the middle of the project, the Atlanta Housing Authority (AHA) scattered the McDaniel Glenn public housing residents across the city as part of Hope VI, a program of the US Department of Housing and Urban Development (HUD) to "deconcentrate poverty." HUD, if you are reading this, maybe next time focus on deconcentrating wealth. The AHA razed the public housing complex with the dubious promise that people could return to new mixed-income housing. Though we tried, we could never keep that group together for the policy advocacy part of the project. From time to time, we would hear from some of them that the banks had foreclosed on their homes and evicted them, even though they had housing vouchers and the housing authority had been paying the rent. The landlords, many of them absentee, pocketed the money but didn't pay the mortgage. The banks didn't care. They still had to go.

With the group that remained in the neighborhood, we formed the Dirty Truth Campaign to expose the truths that Mindy Fullilove describes in her book *Root Shock: How Tearing Up City Neighborhoods Hurts America, And What We Can Do About It*. We enlarged the photos from the project and mounted them at city hall, accompanied by people's stories and analysis. Ronnie and I partnered with a researcher at the Annie E. Casey Foundation Atlanta Civic Site to get us and community residents trained on a protocol to count every single house in the neighborhood and document their condition. We counted 1,296 vacant properties, almost half of the houses in the neighborhood. We took policymakers on a bus tour of the community to witness the levels of vacancy and abandonment that we had documented through the housing census. We petitioned the Casey Foundation to invest in housing, and in response, they developed a land trust and bought and renovated houses for placement in the trust. Belinda, who eventually came around to be all right with me, moved into one of those houses.

After months of coffee and lunch meetings and sorting through pictures on Ronnie's living room floor, a relationship that had begun between two very different humans—a buttoned-up introverted researcher and a gregarious extroverted community organizer—blossomed into a life partnership. We got married a year later. Eventually, the three-year grant expired, but Ronnie and I committed ourselves to the community and bought a house in the neighborhood so we could live where we organized. Organizing and advocacy on a shoestring budget was tough, but there was so much power and love in it as we worked alongside residents of this community to give voice and visibility to the living conditions driving poor health and mental health.

I left Atlanta over a decade ago, but the time I spent in NPU-V is still the most profound, deeply humbling experience of my life. I did bring my training in participatory research and my experience in the Photovoice methodology to the table, but this community taught me about what life was like for Black people battling the debilitating impacts of racialized poverty and trying their damnedest to shine a light on what they were experiencing. As much as I might care deeply about the people behind the statistics, my advocacy is not likely to have the same urgency as theirs. As someone with class privilege, I am too comfortable. All my bills are paid. My belly ... full. This is why I cling to my belief that communities on the margins need to be at the center of their own change efforts. The bottom line is this: they have the most to gain if and when the change they seek comes and the most to lose if it doesn't. Someone with class privilege like me should never be at the center of their change efforts.

GUIDING QUESTIONS:

- How comfortable are you giving up your own power to those at the margins of society so they can lead their own change efforts?
- What would it take for you to deepen your trust in processes that support this?

---

1. Many of the stories in this essay took place within the context of a research project. Therefore, all community members' names have been changed to protect their privacy.

PART II
THEM

5

NOT THAT BLACK

It goes without saying that the racial reality of people of color is different than that of white Americans.
—Derald Wing Sue, *Race Talk and the Conspiracy of Silence*

I CAN FEEL MY HEART BEATING AGAIN. THIS TIME, KAREN HAS COME into my office with a picture of her granddaughter, whom she adores. She points her phone in my direction. "She doesn't look *that* Black, right?" A toddler smiles back at me from the screen. She is adorable. She has a vanilla complexion with warm undertones, twinkling brown eyes, and barely curly brown hair. She is part Black, part white, and part indigenous. That's because Karen's husband is Native American and the mother of her granddaughter is Black. But it's true—her granddaughter Lizzy can easily pass as white, at least for now.

I am at a loss for words. There is a knot in my throat. It is hard to speak or swallow. What does someone Black say in response to a question like this, a question whose very premise is that the appearance of Blackness is undesirable? She unloads about her parents not accepting Lizzy. She says Lizzy's hair, which is soft and wispy, is not too curly, right? The instinct to diminish Lizzy's Blackness is in response to her parents. She had described them as racist and conservative, two facts that bothered her and alienated her from her family. I do feel bad for Karen[1]. She loves her granddaughter, but her parents loathe the fact that she is not fully white.

Karen is strategic and has a critical eye. I appreciate working with her because of this. She is my confidant on executive-level matters, especially the declining endowment, a leftover from the 2008 recession. She is an irritable person, though. She often laments about her husband and her young adult son and daughter. But I am always warmed by her constant rant about some social issue or another. She wears her progressive leanings like a badge of honor. She houses homeless young people—of any race—who need a place to stay. This is more than I can say for myself. My tendency is to support through my professional endeavors. Each time she helps the underdog, I imagine her flicking the middle finger at her parents.

I had worked hard over my life to diminish my own Blackness, struggling for years to accept my own curly hair, broad nose, thick lips, and medium brown skin in a society that despised all these "typical" features of Blackness. I remember the frustrating efforts in middle and high school to keep my hair straight, which started with the hairdresser applying petroleum jelly along the edges of my forehead and the nape of my neck and adding crème relaxer to the new hair growth near the scalp as I sat in her swivel chair. Then, sitting elsewhere in the salon, I persevered through the relaxer's tingling and then burning sensation while waiting thirty minutes for the hair to straighten, during which time scabs would form on my scalp. After that came an under-hood deep conditioning, followed by blow drying, flat ironing, and end-bumping. In between each phase, there were three, sometimes four, other girls or women undergoing the same procedure. All this meant I spent six hours at the beauty salon on a Saturday, at best. Only to repeat the process six weeks later, disciplining the curly hair springing up from the scalp.

I also remember late in high school when I began contouring both sides of my nose with darker shades of foundation and running a lighter color down the bridge to make my nose appear straighter, an illusion I copied from Whitney Houston's look on the cover of the *Bodyguard* soundtrack CD. I no longer contour, but I still catch myself in the mirror or on the screen during Zoom calls examining my nose, always with the question, Is it too big?

Before this conversation with Karen, she and I had talked about the oft-quoted study of racial discrimination in the hiring process, in which résumés with Black-sounding names get callbacks for interviews less frequently than résumés with white-sounding names. I had admitted to her my fear that if our endowment continued to decline because of the recession, I would struggle to find a job because my name with its hard *q* sound would be a dead giveaway of my race on a résumé. This was before LinkedIn and my growing profile in the sector, when I still had a bit of anonymity. She disagreed but not with my belief that I might not find a job. She casually offered that my name sounded French, so she wouldn't assume I was Black. I looked at her through the corner of my eye, my brows furrowing. She had clearly missed the point. It wasn't important to me that my name sound white. What I wanted was for my Blackness not to disqualify me from securing an interview. I didn't say a word. I was stunned into silence, as I so often am. And by the way Karen, just as many Black people as white people speak French globally, thanks to colonialism.

I decide to confront Karen about the question she posed to me about her granddaughter's race. My executive coach facilitates the conversation between us about this microaggression. Her face turns bright pink, and she staunchly denies she ever asked me that question about her granddaughter as I sit in shock and disbelief.

She digs in even further and reveals, of her own volition, that she does not agree with the basic premise of the foundation that racism is the central driver of health inequities. She believes society has a class problem, and if we dealt with poverty and work conditions, people of color would thrive.

"Now it all makes sense!" I exclaim. I had assumed up until this point that her social justice leanings meant commitment to the foundation's racial equity mission. Following our conversation, I initiate a professional development program to see if I might help her develop a race *and* class analysis. From the foundation's perspective, race and class cannot be untethered in the American context. She had recently launched a research effort that brought her out from behind her computer and its spreadsheets into rooms with other funders working to tackle inequities. She needs to be able to communicate the intersection of racism and classism to external audiences.

I plan for us to watch five videos from the *Putting Racism on the Table* series about structural racism, white privilege, implicit bias, mass incarceration, and the impact of racism on all people of color and meet monthly to discuss them. I also plan for her to get individual coaching on how to articulate the centrality of racial equity in the foundation's work. After the second session, she resigns.

This was yet another instance in which I failed to call out racist behavior immediately, and my recounting later was called into question or flatly denied. Derald Wing Sue's book *Race Talk and the Conspiracy of Silence* suggests that fruitful conversations about race may require that people of color call out problematic remarks on the spot for this very reason. White people live a different racial reality and are not as attuned as people of color to the subject of race in conversations. If we let these behaviors slide, white people will miss them and will later say the incidents never happened.

Karen could ask me about whether her granddaughter looked *that* Black and then deny she did because she lives a different reality, one in which hair straightening and nose contouring don't exist. But why should I be responsible for calling out racist behavior or comments on the spot? Can I have a moment to recover from the assault? To catch my breath? To slow down my heartbeat? Tell me. If I decide to come forward later, how could any reasonable person say I fabricated this story from thin air?

GUIDING QUESTIONS:

- Who was the first white woman to diminish your Blackness? Say her name out loud to yourself.
- Have you said her name out loud before? If not, why not?

---

1. This name has been changed to protect details that may impact Lizzy, which is also a fictional name.

6

SUNSHINE AND PAIN

> No woman is responsible for altering the psyche of her oppressor, even when that psyche is embodied in another woman.
> —Audre Lorde, National Women's Studies Association Conference, 1981

I LOVE CLOTHES. ACTUALLY, I HAVE A LOVE-HATE RELATIONSHIP WITH them. I have built my identity around racial justice, so fashion feels frivolous, a guilty pleasure I don't deserve to enjoy until no Black person is struggling. But still I can't resist fashion. I love the drama of runway shows and the red carpet. Well into adulthood, I sat glued to the television for each season of *America's Next Top Model* and *Project Runway* with my teenage daughter on the couch next to me. When I think about my mom's mom, whom I never met, and her love of sewing, the guilt subsides. I tell myself it must be in my genes. Before the COVID-19 pandemic, when I used to travel a fair amount, I would stop in the airport bookstore and grab anything with fashion pages—*Essence*; *O, The Oprah*

Magazine; *InStyle*; and *People Style Watch*—to occupy my heart on flights. I have a love-hate relationship with some of the magazines too. I wish more women who looked like me were represented on the pages.

Midflight, you could find me studying each page as though I were preparing for a test, folding the upper corners of pages containing looks I wanted to replicate. I would then go home and search through my closet to see what I had, the way my wardrobe consultant had shown me when I first got the job at Consumer Health Foundation (CHF). She called it "closet shopping." I had hired her because I wanted to look the part of president and CEO, whatever that is. I would complete the outfit by hunting for a piece at TJ Maxx or shopping online at Nordstrom, where I might "splurge" a bit. Splurge is in quotes because I could never bring myself to truly do it. So many people were counting on me to be judicious with my spending. There is always someone in my network with a need.

One particular "almost splurge" piece (if you call $150 a splurge) was a saffron-colored jacket from a British company called Boden. I had actually purchased two jackets, the other in a color they called fallen fruit. The confirmation email affirmed my choices, saying, "We like your style!" I waited in anticipation for their arrival. I planned to wear one of them to the Washington Regional Association of Grantmakers (WRAG) annual meeting, where I would be introducing the esteemed racism and housing scholar Richard Rothstein at the business meeting of WRAG members.

When the jackets arrived, I pulled them out of the box. I was in love! I paired the saffron-colored jacket with one of my favorite blouses—a deep burgundy number with an oversize pussy bow, a style that symbolized women's entry into corporate America in the 1950s (white women, that is) and the same style that Melania Trump had worn the night of her husband's 2016 presidential debate. Pundits saw it as a taunt after her husband got excoriated for his grab 'em by the pussy "boys' talk." I added an off-white pencil skirt and fall-inspired block-heeled shoes. You couldn't tell me nothing in that outfit! And I planned for my remarks to be just as polished.

I strolled into the grand foyer of the MGM National Harbor hotel and casino the morning of the meeting. I couldn't take my eyes off the huge art installation in the atrium. How much money had they spent on this exhibit? I found the room where the business meeting was taking place and walked down the aisle toward the stage. The current white woman chair of the WRAG board, Lynn, looked me up and down, taking stock of the ensemble, as she greeted me in her typical boisterous, deeply southern way: "Hi, Sunshine!"

Lynn, a tall stocky woman with brassy blond hair, was one of the largest contributors to the annual meeting. She had initially resisted the *Putting Racism on the Table* effort that Tamara Copeland, the Black president of WRAG, and I had been championing. She and I were not friends, though we were cordial, maybe even friendly. "You look like sunshine today in that yellow jacket." I know a compliment when I feel one. This didn't feel good, but I couldn't figure out why. I just felt queasy around her.

When I think of what southern slaveholding women might have been like, it is Lynn whom I see and feel. I know this is a tough comparison to say out loud, but the slaveholding mistress archetype is a truth that lives in the psyche of many Black people. And it's not just Lynn's accent and the fact that she lives in Virginia. It's her resistance to the work on racism, pounding her fist on the WRAG boardroom table as she made the case that we shouldn't host the series because we lacked measurable outcomes. Being around her reminds me of the visceral reaction I have when I drive into any rural area (in the American South or not), and my husband Ronnie and I lock eyes knowingly. Both of us thinking,

Our people were here in distress not too long ago. Are we safe? But I greeted Lynn with a smile and stepped away to find a seat before people started filing in.

I took my seat at the front of the room, and thirty minutes later, when everyone was seated, Lynn kicked off the meeting from the podium. She did try hard to evince sincerity when she talked about her grandchildren playing with Black children. Did she just choke up? I couldn't believe this was all she could muster after all the association talk on structural racism as opposed to interpersonal racism. I was embarrassed for her but continued to hold my face together as I tried to hide the mild irritation and pity I felt as I looked up at her intently.

When it was time to introduce me, she did something completely unexpected: she welcomed me to the stage as Sunshine. Laughter reverberated throughout the room as I tried desperately to contain my self-consciousness. *Ha ha ha ha ha. Ha ha ha ha ha ha.* My heart jumped wildly in my chest. My mind was shutting down as I trod toward the stage. My block heels felt heavy. If I could just get to the podium, I could hold on and steady myself and do what I have trained myself to do in front of white audiences—smile, pull my shoulders back, hold my head up, and deliver with poise, even though I felt like a mouse lost in a maze.

I introduced Richard Rothstein as planned. I told him how personally grateful I was for his scholarship, and within a few minutes, I was back at my seat. I could now collect myself and put Lynn behind me. "Thank you for that introduction, Sunshine," rolled off Rothstein's tongue. He chuckled, and the room was in stitches again. *Ha ha ha ha ha. Ha ha ha ha ha. Ha ha ha ha ha. Ha ha ha ha ha.* I joined in the laughter, though I rolled my eyes and shook my head. Nothing here was funny, but what was there to do but participate in my own humiliation?

What may have seemed like a harmless joke was now a full-on erasure of my name—Dr. Yanique Redwood. It is a name I worked hard to win back after my divorce from my first husband, a name preceded by a title I worked even harder to attain. From what I can determine, not even the accomplished white man standing before us had earned this title. If I stood up now, my legs serving as scaffolding to hold me up amid the laughter, and yelled, "My name is Dr. Yanique Redwood, not Sunshine!" I might as well have walked out of the room and joined a traveling circus. That's how bizarre that scene would be.

In reality, my butt remained parked in the chair. I crossed my legs, gently folded my arms across my lap, and looked up at the podium. I toggled among a range of emotions. I wanted to cry. I wished I could leave the meeting, go home and curl up under my blanket, and take the rest of the day off. At the same time, I was riveted by Richard Rothstein's presentation on the deliberateness of government-sponsored housing segregation and its devastating impacts on Black people. I was also incensed at Lynn. Later that afternoon, I ran into her in the restroom, and she said assuredly, "I hope calling you Sunshine was okay." Was that a question or a statement? The bathroom was busy. It felt like Grand Central Station at rush hour. I was working to get a stain out of my skirt, or else I might have finally stood up for myself, right there in the bathroom of the MGM National Harbor.

That night, I drafted a post about the experience for CHF's blog and shared it with a few people to get feedback. I thought to myself, Am I overreacting? Tamara, the president of WRAG at the time, seemed to think so. She told me her own story of wearing a yellow outfit and being embarrassed when her cousins told her she looked like a banana. I didn't think her example was even close to my situation, but it was enough to sow doubt. I shared the blog with Lynn as a heads-up. But when she apologized after reading it, she followed up with certitude, "I can assure you it had nothing to do with your race. I utilize humor to get people to relax in settings like the annual meeting, where we are all attempting to connect." She didn't acknowledge that she might have caused harm (as Richard Rothstein later did). Even though I had my doubts, I published the blog anyway. I felt more confident doing so after seeking the counsel of Marta Esquilin, a scholar of color who affirmed that what I had experienced was indeed a microaggression.

Marta shared one definition of microaggression with me: a communication that subtly excludes, negates, or nullifies the thoughts, feelings, or experiential reality of a person with marginalized identities. Even if Lynn didn't recognize the harm in the moment she caused it, I expected her to acknowledge upon being confronted that she has no idea what it's like to live in Black skin. It was not until I read Robin DiAngelo's *White Fragility: Why It's So Hard for White People to Talk about Racism* years later that I was able to fully grasp the depth of what had happened. In her book, DiAngelo, a white woman, describes her experience of racial belonging. "In virtually every situation or context deemed normal, neutral, or prestigious in society, I belong racially. This belonging is a deep and ever-present feeling that has always been with me" (2020, 53). I read those words and wondered what that must feel like. I have never had that experience and certainly didn't have it at the WRAG meeting.

Lynn's certainty that her use of humor was well-intentioned and would have the universal outcome that she hoped for is an example (in my opinion) of what DiAngelo refers to as white people's reliance on intention versus impact when confronted with the latter—a way to declare, "I am not a racist." Lynn's words also suggested an adherence to a belief that her experience of the world and my experience of it are the same, thus reinforcing the centrality of whiteness. She never asked questions about what that incident might have meant for me. What it is like to be one of a few. What it is like to code-switch day in and day out. What it means to have your name erased.

For the first time, Tamara, who was a consistent supporter of my work, didn't retweet my blog. I know Tamara was juggling a lot—Lynn was the chair of her board and therefore her boss and one of WRAG's largest sponsors. I didn't take it personally. Black people can do little wrong in my eyes; we are constantly under pressure to make impossible choices. What I did feel, however, was bullied by Lynn. DiAngelo calls white people's responses to racial challenge a form of bullying, explaining that "the effects of our responses are not fragile at all; they are quite powerful because they take advantage of historical and institutional power and control. We wield this power and control in whatever way is most useful in the moment to protect our positions. ... If we need to argue, minimize, explain, play devil's advocate, pout, tune out, or withdraw to stop the challenge, then we will" (2020, 112).

In retrospect, I have greater clarity about what happened that day. The assessment of the clothes on my body has happened before, when I think about the flood of interactions with white women over my life. White women don't know what to do or say around me, so they make comments about my hair, my clothes, my body, my skin, how I talk, or how young I appear. They look me up and down. And then back up again. Akin to my experience with street harassment by Black men, I am objectified by white women. I believe it's what Lynn was doing because we have nothing of any consequence to talk to each other about. Our lives are that far apart. In my opinion, she couldn't see *me*, so she latched on to the yellow jacket on my body.

Actually, it's not that she *couldn't* see me. I believe Lynn refused to see me as her equal. I don't know if Lynn would accept that my skin, if pricked, would hurt in the same way as hers. That although I may look young, I feel as if I have lived many lifetimes. That I am tired to the bone. That my clothes are largely there as a buffer, my hairstyles a wall of defense. So is my PhD that I completed, after dropping out of my program, only so that people would acknowledge me at decisionmaking tables.

I wonder if Lynn knows that it takes effort to make myself smaller and less threatening every day. That it made me feel even smaller when she conducted an orchestra of giggles, chuckles, grins, and snickers at my expense. That this experience felt intentional, a very public yet subtle way of shrinking the Black woman teaming up with Tamara to put racism on the table, an issue she made clear should never have been on it. My experience with Lynn is behind me, but I do have something to say to all the white women who have exploited, discredited, bullied, or erased Black women throughout American history: I emphatically say, "No, it's NOT okay to call us Sunshine, or Mammy, or Girl. Call us by our names."

GUIDING QUESTIONS:

- What has been your experience of microaggressions and/or white fragility in your relationships with white women?
- Have you ever been objectified by white women? If so, what happened?

7

TOKEN

> [When you are a token,] you exchange your rage at inequality for the respect and admiration of your peers. ... You stop pointing out the ways in which people are hurting you or making your identity feel impossible, and unless it is self-serving, you stop pointing out the fact that you are the only one like you.
> —Jacob Tobia, *Sissy*

CHAD, AN OLDER WEALTHY WHITE MAN, LAUNCHED PHILANTHROPY Partners for Women (PPW) in 1995 to provide financial advice to wealthy donors with an interest in gender equity[1]. Some of the largest US-based foundations have relied on PPW's services for their work on issues such as the gender pay gap. Because of his groundbreaking work in the sector, Chad had been invited to serve on the board of the Washington Regional Association of Grantmakers (WRAG). Mary, the white president of a national foundation based in DC, also served on the board of WRAG. Chad's term was ending as mine and Mary's were beginning, and during that overlap, we volunteered to think together about how the association might expand its membership to include individually wealthy donors.

The three of us went to lunch together to begin our brainstorm. Chad chose a restaurant with items on the menu like tartine and chicken liver paté. Even eating with white people at their restaurants makes me nervous. What is a tartine, and why was I the only Black person in this place? The conversation started out benign enough but quickly turned. Chad said he was not happy with WRAG's financial situation under the leadership of its CEO, Tamara Copeland, who is Black. Each year for the past few years, the board had approved an unbalanced budget, and Tamara's efforts to find new revenue opportunities were not producing results fast enough. Mary, who had promised a donation to WRAG to invest in something consequential, expressed her irritation that her foundation's donation had not been activated. There I was at lunch with two powerful white people who might one day help me personally and professionally, and I felt as if I were subtly being roped into validating an unspoken agenda. I kept steering the conversation back to our purpose, and as soon as I got back to my office, I let Tamara know what had happened. She wasn't surprised. She had sensed their disapproval of her leadership. (I will return to Mary in future essays. The rest of this story is about two white men and my growing disillusionment with the philanthropic sector.)

Soon after that lunch conversation, Chad sent me an email invitation to join the PPW board. I was honored to be considered but a bit taken aback. I had little experience with finance and said as much. In my follow-up call with Chad and PPW's new white man director of operations, Steve, they convinced me that my programmatic work in philanthropy would benefit the organization. I was skeptical but agreed to join with the hope that I might have access to influential people who could help Consumer Health Foundation (CHF) advance its racial equity agenda. I didn't mention how concerning it was that no one on the board was a person of color.

Before the first board meeting, Chad, an avid golfer, invited me and my husband, Ronnie, to join him and friends on the greens one weekend. I found a way to weasel out of going. I don't spend my weekends and evenings with white people. It is a boundary I created long ago to keep microaggressions out of my personal life. But I only avoided this outing temporarily. As a part of the first board meeting, PPW board members and some staff members, all white except Phillip, the other Black person joining the board, and me, went golfing followed by dinner. I had never been golfing, and while Tiger Woods is a household name, golfing at a work event was a foreign notion to me. I was super uncomfortable with the entire experience, though I lied afterward and said I had a great time and felt right at home. The whole experience felt quintessentially white and wealthy.

At dinner afterward, Chad introduced me and Phillip and said, with eyes downturned and uncharacteristic meekness, something like "Our donors have been concerned about the lack of board diversity." Diversity often means adding people of color to the mix. And Chad and Steve had done just that. But no one said anything about inclusion—no words to the effect that we would be valued and welcomed and that they would examine the organization's culture to determine how it might impact our ability to thrive. No one said anything about deeper fundamental change needed at the organization to confront legacies of racism that would promote racial equity. At least Phillip was a finance guy, so it made sense why he was there. With Chad's introduction, I felt reduced to a fix for their diversity problem, and I experienced an isolation greater than I had endured on the golf course.

After a couple of board meetings, I raised the idea of tackling racial equity internally, and Chad and Steve took me to lunch to hear me out. Racial equity might mean analyzing PPW's processes to see how they were promoting positive outcomes for women of color or at the very least not causing harm or unintended consequences. Chad is the kind of white man who exudes wealth and accomplishment in ways that make me uncomfortable, but at least he had ideas. I felt that he would understand what I was trying to activate. Steve, on the other hand, seemed out of place. Though well educated, with Ivy League credentials, he came off as another ordinary white man in a position of power. I dreaded my one-on-one meetings with him; I felt as if I were being managed by someone who had little to offer.

During our lunch, I made the case that racial equity work needed to be intentional, not simply an assumed by-product of progressive projects, and suggested that our first step be a racial equity 101 training at our upcoming board meeting. Chad chuckled and said he would need a drink after a conversation about race. I didn't laugh in response. I looked him directly in the eyes and asked him to say more. This was a trick I had picked up from Derald Wing Sue's book *Race Talk and the Conspiracy of Silence: Understanding and Facilitating Difficult Dialogues on Race*. It was a way to challenge white people in the moment on issues of race. According to the book, I was supposed to be sincere in my question, but what I really thought was, If I drank alcohol every time I had to deal with race, I would not have a job allowing me to sit here in front of you two as you try to talk me out of dealing with a topic I can never avoid. I began to feel like this lunch meeting was not to hear me out but to manage me. Chad attempted to explain that racism was a tough topic, but the confrontation had gotten the best of him as he squirmed to respond.

By the end of our lunch, I had been successful in getting them to agree to bring in a racial equity facilitator, the late Avis Ransom, to our upcoming board meeting in Dayton, Ohio. I looked forward to what might unfold. But during the two-day board meeting, I watched as a conversation that was supposed to be about racial equity turned into something else entirely. The conversation slipped into other forms of equity, and the values we adopted out of that conversation sounded as if we were creating marketing materials. I was disgusted. What happened to racial equity? They put my face on their website, which would certainly appease their donors who had woken up and wanted diversity, but they didn't want my perspective on racism. I felt like a token—an acceptable Black person recruited for the appearance of equity.

I checked out emotionally but didn't resign immediately. PPW had set aside $10,000 for each board member to give to an organization of our choosing, and I was committed to getting that money to a law firm working to stem the displacement of Black residents from DC using legal strategies. After the money was out the door, I resigned. I was fed up with the entire sector and quit every board, working group, and committee I was on. Chad and Steve asked for a meeting to talk about it. I declined. I couldn't imagine another lunch with them. I replied to Steve's email: "Thanks for the follow-up. Unfortunately, I don't have the bandwidth for additional conversations, thus part of the reason for my need to resign! I really need to focus on just a few things right now, and I don't think my expertise in racial equity has been a good fit for the PPW board."

GUIDING QUESTIONS:

- Have you ever been in a situation where you felt tokenized? If so, what trade-offs were you making? What power imbalances were you hoping to rectify? What did you gain? What did you lose?

- Have you witnessed another person of color being tokenized? What do you imagine their trade-offs to be?

---

1. I have fictionalized this organization and its leader because of a non-disclosure agreement that I may have signed.

8

A LETTER TO FREDDIE GRAY

Hope
n. The feeling that what is wanted can be had or that events will turn out for the best
v. to look forward to with desire and reasonable confidence
—*Collins English Dictionary*

Dear Freddie,

You don't know me. But I know a little about you from what I heard on the news. In 2015, you were killed in police custody, your spinal cord severed. After you died, your city cried out—erupted, rather—in anger and pain. So a group of people in DC who give away money got scared.

They were afraid that the uprising just an hour away in Baltimore—though it had died down—would find its way to DC. Another Black person would die in police custody, if they did nothing, and it would be like 1968 in DC after Martin Luther King was assassinated. I was in the room with those funders. The foundation I lead gives away money too.

Tamara Copeland, a Black woman who represented about a hundred funders through an organization called the Washington Regional Association of Grantmakers, was the one who brought all of us together to discuss what our response might be. She knew what it was like to talk to her son about the police and wanted to use her platform to do something about police brutality.

She had been shot down by white people when she tried before to talk openly about racism. My colleague Nat Williams suggested that the association say something in response to your death, so I volunteered to write the first draft of the statement. It was clear to me that one of the simplest things we could do was to tell the truth about why this happened to you. Not just the fact that you died but also about the way you lived.

I understand that you had lead poisoning as a child. In my last year of college, I studied the relationship between lead poisoning and children's frustration in school as an intern at the Agency for Toxic Substances and Disease Registry. Lead poisoning is racialized, with Black kids more exposed than white kids, and it likely set you on a trajectory from which you could never return. I believed that if we could just tell the truth about racism and how it puts so many Black people in harm's way, then we could crowd out the lies and stereotypes and things would change for the better.

Though the Orioles enterprise was probably responsible for some of the problems in your city, the owner's son John Angelos also told the truth after you died. He took to Twitter after some complained about the protests disrupting traffic near the ballpark. You weren't even in the ground yet and people wanted their traffic patterns back. John pushed back and said:

"An American political elite have shipped middle class and working class jobs away from Baltimore and cities and towns around the US to 3rd world dictatorships like China and others plunged tens of millions of good hard working Americans into economic devastation and then followed that action around the nation by diminishing every American's civil rights protections in order to control an unfairly impoverished population living under an ever-declining standard of living and suffering at the butt end of an ever-more militarized and aggressive surveillance state. The innocent working families of all backgrounds whose lives and dreams have been cut short by excessive violence, surveillance, and other abuses of the bill of rights by government pay the true price, an ultimate price, and one that far exceeds the importance of any kids' game played tonight, or ever, at Camden Yards."

Setting aside the fact that John didn't name Black people explicitly, he was calling out the structures that led up to your death, and I believed we could do the same with our statement.

Freddie, your death created an opening! Though your death should never have happened, change was on the horizon following your fatal encounter with the police. We anchored the statement on Washington Post writer Michael Fletcher's suggestion that the problems in Baltimore were not primarily racial because its leaders were Black. As if a couple of generations of Black leadership could erase centuries of systemic racism!

We stated in our 692-word piece that 'the sophistication of racism is that it does not need whites, nor does it need malicious intent in order to create negative outcomes for Black people and other people of color,' and that we were certain that what happened in Baltimore was primarily racial and could very easily happen here in the nation's capital.

After defining racism in the statement and offering a few statistics to support our assertion that what happened to you was primarily racial, we made the point that racism is systemic and that addressing racial inequities in our region—and across our country—will require solutions born of an analysis that acknowledges the systemic, not the individual, way in which racism operates.

Yes, the fact that you lived in poverty also contributed, but racism is a root cause of poverty. We closed by saying, 'If racism saps the strength of the whole society through the waste of human resources, it is our contention that all of us will prosper when all people in all neighborhoods have the opportunity to thrive.' Fairly inoffensive, right?

About three weeks after you died, I shared the statement by email with the group of funders. You were dead and your city was crying out, and yet some members of the group thought the statement was too strong. I don't think anyone would say that today. Because of George Floyd's death and the Black Lives Matter protests after he was killed, most people in philanthropic circles will publicly acknowledge racism even as they privately resist efforts to dismantle it.

(By the way, George Floyd was killed in 2020 after a police officer knelt on his neck for nine minutes. It was all caught on camera. The cop was convicted, but we held our collective breath as the jury deliberated. As you know, police brutality, even when caught on camera, most always goes unpunished. In your situation, all the cops got off.) But at that time, few in the sector were willing to publicly challenge systemic racism.

Things got quiet, so Tamara and I convened most everyone on a conference call to talk it out. One by one, each person representing a foundation said they could not sign it. The only grantmakers willing to sign were Consumer Health Foundation (CHF), which is the foundation I was leading, DC Trust, and Hill-Snowdon Foundation. It would not have been powerful enough with just us three, so the statement quietly fluttered to the cutting-room floor.

Mary, a white woman leader, called me up after that deflating conference call to pepper me with questions about what I was trying to accomplish. By the way, this is the same Mary who, a few months prior, appeared to be discrediting Tamara at a lunch meeting that was supposed to be about raising funds for WRAG.

She ended our conversation by saying, 'I just don't think the statement was very strategic.' It was the ultimate insult in philanthropy, a sector that prides itself on smart people sitting around a table making 'strategic' decisions. I have come to believe that when a white person in philanthropy says to a person of color that something they want to do is not 'strategic,' it often means that the person disagrees with the strategy because it disrupts some status quo from which they benefit. It's a common way that white people in philanthropy control our aspirations for freedom and what it takes to get there.

When funders gathered again to decide what to do after my failed attempt to get us to tell the truth about what happened to you, Nicky, the white woman leader of the Meyer Foundation, introduced a quote: 'The first step of leadership is not action, it's understanding.' I quietly disagreed. I believe we can understand while acting, but the quote became the strategy. Before we could address racism, the group decided we needed to learn about racism. As the youngest leader at the table, and still bruised from Mary's phone call, I said nothing. Mary's disapproval mirrored what I had believed about myself all along—you are not good enough, not smart enough. I imagine you may have felt this way at some time in your own short life. Not many Black people get to escape that feeling.

Instead of acting, the group developed a six-month speaker series: Putting Racism on the Table. It dealt with subjects such as structural racism, white privilege, and implicit bias. It was reserved for trustees and CEOs, who had the most power in philanthropy but were also the least likely to acknowledge racism or support efforts to dismantle it.

Even though I didn't agree that learning had to take place first, I was happy to see the sector take this on. My foundation contributed $15,000 and championed the project. Philanthropy was at least starting to reckon with racism, and I was really hopeful, Freddie. CHF had been one of few foundations tackling racism at the local level, and now everyone was finally paying attention.

When the series was announced, a colleague who had formerly been in the DC philanthropic sector called me to say this was a navel-gazing effort by philanthropy. I agreed with him to some extent but was also a bit miffed. Why did he have to be so doubtful? You were in my mind the whole time, Freddie. So young, only twenty-five. Right before you died, it was Eric Garner. Remember him? He was older than you at the time of his death and was hustling to get by, selling cigarettes to make ends meet before a cop choked him to death in broad daylight.

Right after Eric, it was Michael Brown. He was younger than you, eighteen. He was just a kid. Gunned down in the street because he was accused of stealing some cigarillos from a convenience store. Since then, we are still waiting for justice for Breonna Taylor, sprayed with bullets while sleeping. Maybe, just maybe, we could prevent this from happening again if our sector could organize itself and use our power and influence to end the constant assault on Black life. Foundation boards of trustees have people on them who are connected to and inside halls of power. If they shifted, things could really change. I wanted it so badly. Why couldn't my colleague celebrate with me? Couldn't he see that change was coming?

I remember the first day of the series. Eighty-two foundation leaders had registered. I was so excited. When I walked into the conference room, I was struck by the number of white people. I am not sure what I expected. I knew philanthropy was white, but because I spent so much time inside my own foundation, where most people are not white, I had a distorted view of the sector.

A piece of me started to lose hope, seeing all those white faces. I thought, This is going to be an uphill battle. But we kept at it. White people were waking up and sharing how much they did not know about racism and how it shaped the circumstances of people of color. And they kept coming back. By the end of the six-part series, most people had stayed to learn. I was hopeful, Freddie. Really hopeful.

After the series, when it was time to act, my colleague Nat and I co-led a daylong workshop with series attendees to plan next steps. We formed the Racial Equity Working Group and made plans, one of which was to leverage our collective power to decry the loss of affordable housing in a gentrifying city, which would take us to meetings with the zoning commissioner.

While Rick (my white man cochair) and I were

mobilizing ourselves and the group, his CEO, Nicky, constantly questioned me. It seemed that each time I saw her, she asked, "What is going on with the Racial Equity Working Group?" I wished she would just attend the meetings and get her hands dirty. On one call, she told me that even a Black Meyer employee didn't understand what we were doing. Wow. Did she really use one Black person's opinion to negate the efforts of a totally different Black person?

After Rick left the Meyer Foundation, Hanh, an Asian American woman who was leading the Weissberg Foundation, became the working group's cochair. We set up orientation sessions so that anyone joining the group would know what we were about. One orientation session went particularly badly, however. Jennifer M., a white Jewish woman, said something to the effect that Black people needed to stop whining and do something. I could not believe what I was hearing, particularly from someone Jewish. Even though we conducted monthly new member orientations so that everyone would be on the same page, the group was still filled with people whose main mission seemed to be maintenance of the status quo, in which Black people are constantly trying to make it and, while doing so, die early and unnecessarily.

In addition to Jennifer M., there were others who all seemed to be on a mission to slow the group down. Each time we proceeded to act, such as when we planned to form a speaker's bureau, one of them would say we needed more training, and Hanh and I would scurry to find more training, like the one hosted by Race Forward on narrative change. When we made a statement about anti-Black racism on the anniversary of the Unite the Right rally, two leaders, Julia and Anna, called me up separately to question the statement's lack of inclusivity, particularly of Jewish people. The group had decided to center anti-Blackness, but when it came time to release our statement, I got what felt like questioning, belligerent emails and phone calls.

As I slowly realized this group would never be bold—in either words or action—I experienced a very real foreboding, Freddie. I had been burning the candle at both ends. I was meeting with councilmembers frequently to explain racial equity. I was working hard to influence my peers in philanthropy. I was running an organization and steering them toward a more explicit vision around antiracism and community. I had also tried to host a panel discussion on the legacy of racism in housing with an attorney named Ari Theresa. (By the way, you would have liked Ari. I know you lived in Gilmor Homes at some point in your life. Ari fights for Black people in public housing.)

But one by one, everyone who had signed up as a partner or had been invited to be partner, said they couldn't participate. Some didn't want to upset their donors or board members who had made money through real estate transactions that were likely responsible for the gentrification patterns in the region. One organization's board member was named in a lawsuit that Ari had filed on behalf of residents.

After the planned event fell apart, a researcher of color at the Urban Institute called me up to say that there were other ways to get at the problem without involving someone with a reputation like Ari, whose relentless approach to defending poor Black people made those in the power structure uncomfortable. Calls like these always felt as though I were being schooled on how to keep quiet, whether from leaders of color, who said that I needed to tone down the race talk, or white colleagues, who would never say that out loud, but their actions said it all.

Freddie, I feel bad saying this. But after all that, I was spent. I had started off hopeful but soon realized that the philanthropic sector was willing to go only so far. Even though my white colleagues were waking up to the impacts of racism, they would not give up their power—reputational, financial, or otherwise—to save your life or mine.

That's when I lost all hope. I pray I am not going too far when I say this: the same system that literally broke your back was part of the same racist structure that finally did me in. Freddie, by the time of the third anniversary of your death, I had nothing left to give.

I'm so sorry I let you down.

Yanique

GUIDING QUESTIONS:

- How do you maintain hope in the face of racism's unrelenting attacks?
- What are your perspectives on people of color who give up hope?

9

UNHINGED

> Racism is a visceral experience ... it dislodges brains, blocks airways, rips muscle, extracts organs, cracks bones, breaks teeth. ... The sociology, the history, the economics, the graphs, the charts, the regressions all land, with great violence, upon the body.
> —Ta-Nehisi Coates, *Between the World and Me*

> But while anti-Jewish sentiment is real, White Jews must reckon with the fact that we will never walk in Black skin, that our history in America is nowhere near as devastating as the history of that of Black Americans.
> —Justin C. Cohen, "This Yom Kippur, I'm Atoning for White Supremacy"

MY CELL PHONE RARELY RINGS; MY FRIENDS KNOW I'M NOT ONE FOR impromptu calls. Blame it on the introvert in me. But when my doctor's number flashed on my screen that sunny fall day, I picked up. I had been expecting test results. Recent days had been running together—I had taken two weeks' leave after five years on the job to deal with exhaustion and was moving between sleep and waking.

Nicole, my physician assistant, chirped hello. Her next sentence shifted the energy. "Your test for Lyme disease came back positive." The surprise in her voice matched my own. I couldn't tell the last time I had interacted with a blade of grass, much less fields of the stuff. The closest I had gotten to woods was sitting on my patio overlooking a manicured group of trees the developers had left standing when they carved out our housing development. Sometimes we saw deer in that patch of woods, but a series of unlikely events would have had to occur for a tick to attach to my body.

I had agreed to take a battery of tests a couple of weeks back as a means of ruling out the many horrible diseases that could explain my symptoms—weariness and fatigue so intense I felt as though I might tip over with each step and pain that enwrapped my body. The muscles in my arms, thighs, and legs felt tender and inflamed, and there was a constant ache deep in my knees and in the joints of all my fingers except the thumbs. Ibuprofen provided little relief. The only thing that seemed to work was my husband Ronnie's kneading and squeezing of my muscles and joints as I hissed in agony.

I was certain this was a false positive result, but I consented to a two-week regimen of antibiotics and spent the rest of my time away from the office reading about all the ways in which Lyme disease could ruin my life. Toward the end of the regimen, I saw an infectious disease specialist. I needed a second opinion because it seemed too implausible. He sat on his little stool and asked detailed questions about exposure routes and symptoms as I perched on the edge of the slightly elevated exam table. He listened as I described what I had been experiencing, including the night sweats that left my bed and body soaked and refused to allow me a full night of sleep.

After he finished taking notes, he looked up at me and declared, "You do not have Lyme disease." He said my antidepressant was the likely night-sweat culprit. "But what about the fatigue and body aches?" I asked. He had no answer for that and sent me back to Nicole for follow-up. I did begin to feel better after completing the full course of antibiotics. Feeling better certainly complicated matters. Had it indeed been Lyme and the infectious disease specialist missed it? Or had it been the stress of dealing with a board member, Roberta, over the past six months and my two weeks away from the office simply provided some distance?

Roberta was an older white woman on the Consumer Health Foundation (CHF) Board of Trustees. Essentially, she was one of my eleven or so bosses (the number fluctuates as people roll on and off the board at the end of their terms). She was tall and long-legged and displayed the tell-tale signs of advanced aging—white hair, a shaky voice, and a slight rounding of the upper back. She was a retired healthcare executive with a penchant for nice things —clothes, bags, jewelry, and vacations. I generally had positive working relationships with the trustees who led the foundation at any given time. That was part of the job. Though Roberta and I were from different worlds, I, too, enjoyed beautiful clothes and interesting destinations, so we traded travel stories and compliments on earrings or shoes. But over time, our relationship soured.

At one of our retreats for board and staff members, the facilitator asked us each to tell a story about our first experience with someone of another race to deepen our racial equity analysis. Roberta told a story about her Black nanny and her mother's encouragement to treat Black people well. After we had all told our stories, Roberta, who is Jewish, raised her hand. She suggested to the facilitator that when we talk about white people and their role in racism, we needed to say white Protestants. The facilitator mentioned something about intersections, but all I could think about was Roberta's seeming insinuation that white Jewish people could not be implicated in racism. Yes, white Jews in the sector were often willing to take on issues of racial justice because of their own histories of discrimination both in Nazi Germany and the United States. But I was unnerved by how comfortable she seemed using her Jewishness to conceal her whiteness.

Around the same time, the Washington Regional Association of Grantmakers (WRAG), the association of family, independent, and community foundations and corporate giving programs in DC, hired Holly Bass, a Black performance artist, for its annual meeting, where Harvard professor David Williams presented his talk "The House That Racism Built." She had interviewed four philanthropic leaders, two white and two Black. I was one of the interviewees.

She pieced our stories together, and a DJ used looping and mixing techniques to form the backdrop to her liturgical dance, a dance form commonly seen in Black churches on Sundays. After Dr. Williams's talk met with a loud and extended round of applause, Holly appeared onstage with coiffed natural hair and wearing a long, black sleeveless dress, exposing her dancer's arms. As the recording of our voices played in the background, she moved deliberately across the stage with arms and legs outstretched, conveying through her body the intensity of our views on racism and social change.

I sat enthralled as the performance unfolded. I had not known what to expect when I agreed to be interviewed. The performance then ended with my words, my voice faltering as I attempted to answer her question about how I measure progress: "I just decided that even if I can't see it, the thing that is in my head, where Black people and people of color get to express their full humanity (and I just don't think that's going to happen in my lifetime, as hard as that is to say), I just believe in ... just putting one foot in front of the other ... I don't really spend a lot of time thinking about progress or thinking about the ultimate goal. I just believe that I gotta keep going. I just keep moving."

We all watched her grab the ankle of her left leg with both hands and carry it forward, and then she did the same with her right ankle as I whispered on a loop:

> *Just keep moving.*
> *Just keep moving.*
> *Just keep moving.*

Until the sound faded and she lowered her head.

I played the recording of the performance over dinner before the official start of the next CHF board meeting for those who had not been able to attend. I had been moved by the performance and was compelled to share it. I expected everyone to be as riveted as those of us at the annual meeting had been. After Holly lowered her head, I stopped the video and listened expectantly.

When it was Roberta's turn to speak, she said, "I don't understand that." That was it. Just four words. I eyed her from across the table. She had just heard me articulate a profound sense of hopelessness and that I no longer believed in a theory of change. I kept going, not because I believed my efforts would make a difference but because there was nothing else to do but keep moving. Even if she had missed the cultural cues in the liturgical dance, how could she have heard my voice quiver as I held back tears and not feel something? Anything? She could have kept silent, yet she chose to speak up and, in doing so, my experience felt diminished. I was flattened.

Roberta was already on the board when I joined the foundation in 2012. She was on the search committee that recommended me to become the foundation's second CEO. CHF had a history of leading on the topic of racial equity under the former white CEO.

But I came to make racial equity real in a way that only a Black radicalized woman can. It seemed that each time I tried to move the foundation toward a more explicit focus on racism as the most important predictor of health, Roberta would ask something like, "What does that have to do with health?" The question aggravated me.

It was so obvious to me, and has been confirmed repeatedly by a deep and vast scientific literature, that every social issue is undergirded by racism, and therefore racism predicts health. Food apartheid means that people of color live in communities where healthy food is just not available. The history of redlining means that Black people were collectively blocked from homeownership and the resulting wealth that our white counterparts have been able to use to buy into neighborhoods with high-functioning schools, parks, and safe housing. The lack of living-wage jobs leads to impossible choices such as between food and medicine, and the stress of living in a racist society takes up residence in the body, even for Black people with class privilege like me. I worked hard to maintain my composure each time Roberta lobbed the question. Because she had spent her entire career in healthcare settings, I understood that she was coming to the conversation with different notions about what constitutes health. But something other than her work experience seemed to be at play.

Since my exposure to racial inequity statistics in graduate school—for example, that poor Black women were less likely than white women to live long enough to see their children turn twenty—I became desperate to convince others of the deep-seated nature of racism and the magnitude of unavoidable pain and suffering in Black communities. I learned about this statistic from Arline Geronimus, a tough-as-nails white Jewish professor in my doctoral program. Before taking a class with her, I sought her guidance on the first draft of a paper I had written for one of my introductory public health courses. Her scholarship focused on Black women, so I sought her out because I had written about Black single mothers, their rates of pregnancy and abortion, and interventions, such as birth control, to improve their health and social circumstances. When I sat down in her office, she handed me a printout of the paper with a slew of strike-throughs, revisions, and comments and questions in the margins.

She said my analysis was faulty and steeped in middle-class and religious biases. I had made assumptions about what constituted family (two parents and children), the right timing for childbirth (late twenties and early thirties), and the morality of sex before marriage and abortion (neither should happen), even though at this point my own child had been born outside of marriage when I was twenty-one, an event that was the source of the religiously motivated shame I both carried around and tried hard to bury. She also let me know that these kinds of biases, when applied to Black women, constituted racism and that I needed to rewrite my paper after consulting her Women's Health and the Timing of Reproduction class syllabus. I walked out of her office, first feeling dazed and then filled with righteous indignation. What does a white woman know about Black women? And how dare she suggest that I might be racist? One thing I hate, however, is for someone to see my faults before I do, so I dove into her syllabus and later took her class, which opened me up to truths about the ways in which racism wormed its way into our bodies, shaped life choices, and made us sick.

Dr. Geronimus coined the term "weathering" and explained that Black women's bodies deteriorate faster than white women's bodies, and she hypothesized that this was due to the stress of living in a racist society. Consequently, Black women may not have the choice to wait until their early thirties to have healthy children; their bodies are healthiest in their late teens and early twenties, a socially unacceptable age to have children in the United States. I had superimposed a white supremacist Christocentric worldview onto the women I was claiming to care about. The worst part was that it took a white woman to help me see it. Sometimes I think my desperate attempts to convince others of the centrality of racism comes from the need to purge my own biases. My head knows and understands, but I am afraid of what still lives in my colonized heart.

By the beginning of 2017, the same year that I took time off to reckon with my fatigue, I had to come to terms with the fact that Donald Trump had won the presidency on a platform of white supremacy, a reality that left me bewildered and increasingly unhinged. Not the unhinged that reporters used to describe Trump himself, but the feeling that something dreadful was closing in on me. By summer, the news footage from the Unite the Right rally in Charlottesville, Virginia, looked strikingly like images of white people protesting Black progress in the 1950s and 1960s.

The city of Charlottesville had proposed a reparations package intended to benefit Black people. That package included funding for housing and education, and there was a parallel effort to remove a statue of Confederate general Robert E. Lee from a local park. In response, white supremacists organized to oppose these actions. As I watched white nationalists, neo-Nazis, Klansmen, and right-wing militias marching to protest the removal of the statue, I was gripped by fear—of these white supremacists, yes, but much more so of losing ground in the movement for racial equity and justice in philanthropy. I had been working, along with others in the Racial Equity Working Group of WRAG, to help our peers understand structural racism. This rally was a distraction.

With support from the president of WRAG and my Racial Equity Working Group cochair Hanh Le, I penned a statement on Charlottesville with a focus on anti-Blackness, an issue the working group had agreed to prioritize. I wrote the statement as a clarion call to ignore the clamorous manifestation of racism that had been on display in Charlottesville. I implored, instead, for renewed attention to the quiet ways in which structural racism kills hundreds of Black people daily. I was certain that the impetus for the rally was in response to Blackness, the same way that Trumpism could not have happened without Barack and Michelle Obama posted up in the White House. Thus I did not think for a second to highlight the anti-Jewish sentiments—shouts of "Jews will not replace us!"—that were also part of the rally.

Amid overwhelming support for the statement, a critique came in via email from Alison, the executive director of a local foundation. She said she was speaking on behalf of the Jewish family foundations that were members of WRAG. She called the statement narrow and exclusive because it didn't acknowledge others who had been targeted or left out because of their race, religion, gender, ethnicity, or sexual orientation. She then offered advice about how to write future statements, so sure was she of her position.

How many times had Black people begged for space to simply voice what was happening to us without having to make space for others? Each time a focus on anti-Blackness surfaced at conferences and decisionmaking tables, someone would inevitably ask, "What about _____?" Alison may not have known about this phenomenon or the craving in Black communities to be centered long enough to be fully seen. The situation reminded me of the time I gave a talk about racism at a policy conference and a white woman sprang to her feet toward the end of Q & A and angrily asked, "What about women?" As if I were not a woman. But she wasn't really asking about Black women, was she?

I tried hard to empathize with them both, particularly my philanthropy colleague, but I just couldn't. The statement I had authored was centrally about how hundreds of Black people were dying daily due to racism—a phenomenon that Harvard professor David Williams likens to a jumbo jet taking off from Boston Logan airport and crashing day in and day out every year—yet Alison (and the group of Jewish foundations she said she represented) did not seem to appreciate that white Jewish people in the United States benefit from whiteness and therefore did not need a mention in the context of my thesis about African Americans. Just like Roberta, they seemed to be using the Jewish part of their identity to conceal the privileges of whiteness they enjoyed.

It's why a white Jewish woman in DC-area philanthropy could say to a multiracial group of people while attending a racial justice conference, "If you can say 'white supremacy,' then why can't I say 'nigger'?" Though white supremacists also target Jews, she was offended by the term "white supremacy" and spoke out in defense of her whiteness. What other reason could there be for a Jewish person to want to use the word "nigger"? It's also why another white Jewish woman could touch me on the arm and say to me the day after Donald Trump was elected president of the United States, "I feel sorry for you and your daughter." Although Trump's election unleashed a new wave of anti-Semitism and she, too, should have been afraid, she probably knew deep down that her whiteness would protect her and her two daughters more than my Blackness could ever protect me and mine.

While my heart breaks for Jewish people who still live with fear and vigilance instilled by the experiences of their forefathers and foremothers and as a product of present-day anti-Semitism, my heart breaks even more for Black people who are traumatized daily across the country by an all-too-present and pernicious white supremacist police force that kicks, beats, suffocates, shoots, and kills both children and adults in their own homes, in parks, and on public sidewalks. I seethe about the Black people who suffer every day from racism-related stress that contributes to heart disease and diabetes, rendering us unable to fight off the devastating impacts of new diseases like COVID-19. I can't, and won't, think about the Black people who waste away in cages for charges related to marijuana as white people launch marijuana dispensaries, some lucrative enough to be publicly traded on the stock market. If I think about it, I may not recover from the pain.

Where was the radical empathy that would have allowed my white Jewish colleagues to distinguish between our current plight and theirs, act in ways that brought more attention and resources to the eradication of anti-Blackness, and resist the question "What about others?" I had been away at a healing retreat for Black women in philanthropy when the email came from Alison. I articulated my disappointment, but she dug in. No matter what I said, it didn't make a difference. I cried alone in my room. Why couldn't she see?

At the CHF board meeting before I took two weeks off to deal with my debilitating fatigue, I revealed during my performance review, with tears streaming embarrassingly down my face, that I was having a tough time in the sector, a scene that would recur a year later in my next performance review. I told my board about the Charlottesville statement and the reaction from the Jewish foundations and stated that this was a typical Jewish response in the sector.

In addition, I explained that I regularly suffered through microaggressions. (Scholar and author Ibram X. Kendi says in his book *How to Be an Antiracist* that there is nothing minor about these aggressions and uses the term "racist abuse" instead.) I nervously turned to Roberta and asked permission to share comments that the chair of her civic association, Robin, had recently made about my hair when the three of us met to discuss ways to involve white wealthy DC residents in efforts to advance racial equity. I left out the comment Roberta had made about my articulateness during that meeting, wanting to avoid humiliating her in front of her colleagues for using this famous racist euphemism.

When I was done speaking, Deborah, a Black woman on the

board, said, "Whether you go to heaven or hell, a Black woman will be at the gate to greet you." I didn't understand what she meant, but I knew she was on my side. Silvia, a Latina woman, also lent her support and echoed her own experiences of racial abuse in the sector. She said, "I know what Yanique is talking about." As soon as the meeting adjourned, Roberta cornered me. "Jewish people are oppressed too." Her voice trembled from age and rage. "Jewish people are oppressed too." Her eyes bulged and her body jerked. "Jewish people are oppressed too." I took a step back. She was too close. She seemed unhinged. She would later say this interchange never happened.

I realize this is sensitive commentary. Do white Jewish people experience xenophobia? Absolutely. Have they been oppressed? Yes. Are they still oppressed? Of course. We see this, for example, in the mass shootings at synagogues in recent years—in Pittsburgh, Pennsylvania, in 2018 and in Poway, California, in 2019. Do white Jewish people simultaneously benefit from whiteness? The answer is also yes. Just as white gay men experience oppression because of anti-gay rhetoric and policies, they also benefit from whiteness. This whiteness means that white gay men have a one-in-eleven lifetime risk of HIV while Black gay men have a one-in-two lifetime risk of HIV, according to a study by the CDC (Hess et al. 2017). This almost forty years after white gay men were dropping like flies, a common reference to the number of white gay men who died at the top of the AIDS epidemic in the 1980s. This while Black communities today have the most severe burden of HIV of all racial and ethnic groups in the United States. This is not happenstance.

I have spent two decades since that day in Arline Geronimus's office wrestling with my privilege, gouging out its eyes and the way it sees the world, forcing it to shut up and listen, and at times, finding a way to make peace with it and ultimately giving some of it away. If I can do this as someone in what Isabel Wilkerson terms the "lower caste" in her book *Caste: The Origins of Our Discontents*, then certainly Roberta and my other white Jewish colleagues can do the same. Otherwise, we cause further harm and advocate for programs and policies that center our self-centered worldviews. Refusing to battle with our privilege, even as members of an oppressed group, inevitably means we become an oppressor. We can't have it both ways.

Earlier in the year, in the first board meeting after the election of Donald Trump, trustees Silvia and Darakshan had shared gut-wrenching stories of the fear and trauma in Latino and Muslim communities due to ICE raids and the Muslim ban. I also shared bits of a conversation I'd had with a high-ranking DC government official during a meeting on racial inequities in the district. She had leaned over during a break and had whispered to me about the difficulty of moving a racial equity agenda from inside local government. She said white people in the district had consistently quashed her efforts at equity.

When she tried to convince white parents that more school nurses were needed in the schools where Black children struggled with asthma (an example of equity), these parents insisted on equality—having the same number of school nurses even though their children didn't need them. Her analysis was spot on. Asthma inequities are racialized, resulting from histories of poor housing in communities of color and the construction of highways that cut through Black communities, bringing with them truck and car exhaust and particulate matter. She warned that we needed to get white people mobilized if we were to have any chance at racial equity. Racial equity requires that more or different resources go to those most impacted by racism, and to do this would require that white people finally give up some of what they had been hoarding.

In response, Roberta, who lived in a DC ward along with the wealthiest white residents, said matter-of-factly, "White people want to help, but it is Black people who are committing crimes in my neighborhood." I stiffened and looked around the conference room table for someone to take exception. No one did. Not even me. We all sat in silence. If the late comedian Paul Mooney had been at the table, he would have said, "Shhh. White folks talking."

This board led by a majority of Black people and people of color practiced what author and psychotherapist Resmaa Menakem calls "racial caping," a phenomenon in which Black people work to keep white people calm instead of voicing what needs to be said. He explains, "White comfort always trumps our liberation ... because we know that when white people get nervous, Black people die. When white people get nervous, Black people lose their jobs. When white people get nervous, Black people lose their stature, so we reflexively make moves to calm white people down to protect ourselves and other people" (personal communication, March 25, 2022). But this was the last straw for me. I was done protecting Roberta.

In my email the next day, I thanked Roberta for her comments and then proceeded to explain why they were problematic. "This is not to say that African Americans don't commit crime," I hedged. "All people commit crime, but very rarely are whites monitored as heavily and therefore arrested, adjudicated, and imprisoned for crime." I also shared a link to a Ted Talk that I still watch at least once a year, adding to the 26 million times it has been viewed. In the talk, author Chimamanda Ngozi Adichie schools a mostly white audience on the danger of a single story and introduces an Igbo word *nkali*, a noun that implies power and can be loosely translated as "to be greater than another." She says, "Power is the ability not just to tell the story of another person but to make it the definitive story of that person."

Crime stories about Black people are about power, one of the oldest tricks in the white supremacy playbook. Paint us as dangerous, get enough people to buy into the narrative, and you can guarantee winning most any election on that platform and justify the control, plunder, and deprivation of our "undeserving" communities. I pointed Roberta to *13th*, a Netflix documentary by director Ava DuVernay about the criminalization of Black people and the unconscionable levels of mass incarceration unmatched in the world, a phenomenon that Michelle Alexander also details in her book *The New Jim Crow: Mass Incarceration in the Age of Colorblindness*. Roberta responded with interest in talking further and offered her analysis that her neighborhood's newspaper crime reports usually call out race when a Black person is involved in a crime but not necessarily when the person is white. I was so proud of myself. I had made an impact!

A few months later, Roberta asked to meet with me. She had engaged her civic association chair, Robin, and they wanted to discuss how to involve white people in their wards in a dialogue about racial equity. I eagerly agreed. I was thinking about that government official's counsel: mobilize white people. They also planned to approach their councilmember Jack Evans, an older white man who had been on the DC council for almost thirty years. This is the same Jack who, along with his ally on the council Mary Cheh, looked me in the eyes months later as I co-facilitated a racial equity training for all councilmembers and told me he wasn't giving up anything he had worked hard for in the name of equity. A 2022 *Washington Post* article written by Steve Thompson, stated that "investigations commissioned by the Washington Metropolitan Area Transit Authority board, where Evans served as chair, and the D.C. Council found that he abused his offices to help clients who paid him $400,000 in consulting fees." Yes, such hard work, indeed.

Roberta, Robin, and I met in CHF's rectangular conference room with its deep-orange walls, dim lighting, and a quote by the abolitionist Henry David Thoreau in oversize black block letters bonded to the longer wall: "It's not what you look at that matters, it's what you see." As we exchanged pleasantries, Robin opened by saying that a family member, possibly her father, had marched with Dr. Martin Luther King. This was the first sign of trouble. From my perspective, a white person who leads with their family's legacy of civil rights is a white person who is proving solidarity versus being in solidarity. In hindsight, I should have involved another board member in that meeting. Preferably a white one.

We discussed the possibility that I might deliver a talk on racial equity for the civic association even though Robin disagreed. Then why was she here? She said that the people who lived in the neighborhood were doctors and lawyers, well-educated people who knew what to do to solve society's problems. One of CHF's five elements of a racial equity approach, which borrowed from grassroots movements and movements in the more radical corners of the academy, asserts that impacted communities should design and lead solutions to the challenges in their own communities. Robin and I could not have been farther apart on who should lead. Did she really think that being a doctor or lawyer qualified one to address racism? Roberta jumped in and refuted Robin's assertion. She shared her newly minted insight, an insight she believed her doctor-lawyer neighbors didn't have and thus why they needed racial equity training—that their neighborhood newspaper always named a person's race when the person who committed the crime was Black and was silent on race when the person who committed the crime was white. I beamed. Roberta was becoming an ally.

I suggested Nicky as an alternative speaker. Nicky, a white philanthropic leader, had led the Meyer Foundation through a racial equity transition. I imagined that she might be a better fit for this largely white audience. They tag-teamed to say that it had to be me. Roberta said that I would be a great speaker for this training because I was articulate. I recall the first time this veiled compliment was directed at me. I was in graduate school. Was it a professor or a peer? It's hard to remember. But I recall the feeling.

It felt affirming. It meant that all my efforts to be whitelike had paid off, particularly the way in which I spoke—my diction, my word choices, my pacing, my mannerisms. I began perfecting all of these in high school debate class, including tamping down my Jamaican patois, which caused an inflection at the ends of my sentences. But I also remember not feeling affirmed for very long. I soon understood this statement to be racist—a suggestion that it was rare for a Black person to be articulate. It was also a way to separate those of us who assimilated as a survival strategy from those who refuse to assimilate or those who couldn't assimilate even if they tried.

I confess that I made this statement once—about a Black person's articulateness. It was at the WRAG board meeting, at the beginning of my first term as chair, a meeting attended by the same Nicky I had recommended Roberta and Robin recruit for the talk on racial equity. When it came out of my mouth, I immediately recognized my error. "Humph," Nicky reacted under her breath. She was sitting right next to me, positioned next in line for the role of board chair. I assumed my faux pas prompted her response. Any student of racial equity 101 would have spotted it. I had called Meyer Memorial Trust's chief investment officer Rukaiyah Adams's presentation polished. Rukaiyah had delivered an arresting presentation about the cognitive dissonance she experienced when she discovered that while her foundation gave grants to address affordable housing, it simultaneously invested in real estate investment trusts, which are real estate holdings not available on the market because they are being held until they appreciate and can turn a profit.

One side of her foundation house was attempting to fix an affordable housing crisis, while the other, larger side was *creating* it. I was indeed proud of Rukaiyah—a Black woman serving as chief investment officer of an $800 million private foundation. How many of those existed at the time? One? Two?

Three? Her words were inspiring yet sharp, honest, and vulnerable. I recognized her. She was me. She was my people. And she spoke in ways that white people might be able to hear. That's what I wanted to say. Not that she was less Black, but that she spoke using sound waves that might make it into white people's ears. But instead of saying that, I went for the shorthand—polished.

However, what I believe my board member Roberta implied when she called me articulate was palatability: You are less Black. You are less threatening. Robin followed up and said, "You also have that great haircut." At the time, I was wearing a fade—naturally curly, low on the sides, and slightly higher on top. "Plus, I am a member of the Democratic Women Club and we have a leader of color who speaks to us all the time." They had not only called me articulate, but they also referred to my hair as a qualifier for speaking and had lumped me with another person of color to bolster their pitch for a speaker of color. Beyond skin color, hair might be the single most important identifier of Blackness. The topic is fraught with pain (and more recently, joy) for Black women, even requiring legislation to prohibit discrimination based on hair style or texture, a law in California, Maryland, and 17 other states known as the Crown Act. In my humiliation, I participated in my own oppression. I touched my hair and replied, "Oh you like it? I just got it cut."

When they walked out of the conference room, a wave of sadness and grief washed over me. A feeling of wading through mud crept in. It was August and sweltering, but I took a walk around the block to regain my composure. When I returned to my desk, I could only muster the energy to call Sukari, my executive coach, and then spent the afternoon crying behind my closed door. "It's not what you look at that matters, it's what you see," read the quote on the conference room wall. The only thing I felt they could see was my phenotype. I felt tokenized, a muse for their amusement. Ronnie had a stronger take: "They wanted to see a nigger dance."

In retrospect, the few details about the hair comment that I shared with the board did not paint a full picture of what I had been going through. I didn't share all the details because I was negotiating professionalism—you don't cry in your performance review—and I didn't want to throw Roberta under the bus in front of her colleagues (another example of racial caping). While I tried to spare her, she offered me no such grace. An email from her arrived the next day, and we continued a cat-and-mouse chase by email in the ensuing months.

From: Roberta
Sent: Tuesday, September 26, 2017
To: Yanique
Subject: Comment at the board meeting

Hi Yanique. I would like to talk to you about a comment you made at the board meeting which disturbed and actually upset me. You talked about the pushback and even derogatory comments you received from some people when you were discussing issues of equity. You specifically mentioned as disturbing "the Jewish response." I do not know to what you were referring and would like to. But I am very sensitive to anti-Semitism and am concerned that you or anyone feels that there is one "Jewish" response and that response is prejudiced. Upon reflection I do wish that you had spoken to me about Robin. I am so sorry about that conversation. Roberta

The email unnerved me in its suggestion that I might be anti-Semitic. I had never before been accused of this, and it frightened me. I knew that being called anti-Semitic was on par with being called racist. What does one say or do to be anti-Semitic? I knew some of the stereotypes about Jewish people, but I wondered what I might have missed. I started reading to better understand.

> **From:** Roberta
> **Sent:** Thursday, September 28, 2017
> **To:** Yanique
> **Subject:** Fwd: anti-Semitic literature on stoops in Shaw
>
> Hi. This is why I get upset. It is not you but the environment. Roberta
>
> From: "Nextdoor Dupont Circle" <reply@rs.e-mail.nextdoor.com>
> Sent: September 28, 2017
> To: Roberta
> Subject: anti-Semitic literature on stoops in Shaw
>
> Hey all, Sadly woke up this morning to find anti-Semitic literature left on the doorstep. 8x11 double-sided sheet. Appeared to be on every stoop on French Street NW. Curious how far and wide this was. And if anyone with camera/video might have seen who was dropping them off (sometime between 7-8am 9/28 on my block). I'll do my best to attach the image - but had a Dr. Bronner's, handmade feel.

When I got this second email, I felt even more afraid. I didn't think I alone could address Roberta's distress and reflexive reaction to the broader environment. We needed a strong facilitator to help us have this sensitive conversation.

> **From:** Yanique

Sent: Tuesday, October 3, 2017
To: Roberta
Subject: Meeting

Hi Roberta,

Thanks for reaching out. Given how much we are both struggling with these issues, I have reached out to someone at the Anti-Defamation League who does work with Black and Jewish communities. I will be meeting with him this week to get his advice on the most constructive way to have this conversation. I spoke with David about the possibility of the board having a brown bag lunch discussion this fall, and he was supportive. What do you think? Would you be open to this? Yanique

From: Roberta
Sent: Tuesday, October 3, 2017
To: Yanique
Subject: Meeting

Yanique. I just want to talk with you to understand the comment you made and the context. It may be nothing more than how you phrased what you said and my response to it. I do not feel that there is any pervasive anti-Semitic feeling at CHF or on the board. Let's just talk and figure it out. Is that OK? Roberta

From: Yanique
Sent: Tuesday, October 3, 2017
To: Roberta
Subject: Meeting

Dear Roberta, It would be helpful for me to talk to the person that I mentioned first. I am not reaching out to him because I believe there is pervasive anti-Semitism in the organization. I think there are some deeper issues at this intersection that he might be able to help us to discover. It would also help us to lead. This tension is also present in the nonprofit community and in philanthropy, and there is little being done to address it. I will circle back to you after I have met with him and after I have taken some time off to process all of this. Like I said, it has been a difficult summer. If you would like to know the context, I can give you a quick call right now to share it. Please let me know your phone number. Yanique

I called Roberta and immediately apologized for any suggestion that there was only one Jewish response. Taking the action of one person of an oppressed group and applying it broadly to the group is one aspect of racism and xenophobia. "However," I said, "I have experienced on several occasions the 'What about us?' question from Jewish colleagues." This observation was not anti-Semitic. She was not satisfied with my apology and still wanted to meet.

I suggested that we needed support.

She said she simply wanted to talk.

I said I didn't feel safe.

She went to my board chair.

David, one of two Black men on the board and chair of the board at the time, forwarded the email she had sent to him demanding an individual conversation with me. At my suggestion, he discussed with her the benefits of using a facilitator, and she agreed to proceed with one. Roberta and I met individually with the late Avis Ransom, a Black facilitator with Baltimore Racial Justice Action who had experience engaging white people, before the planned date of the joint meeting. But Roberta resigned from the board shortly thereafter. She told David that her meeting with Avis had made things worse.

The clash between Black and Jewish people was not new. Just that summer, CHF had supported a facilitated conversation between Jews United for Justice (JUFJ) and Black organizers in DC who had released an open letter to JUFJ. The Black organizers believed that JUFJ's "organizing praxis was mainly transactional and resulted in their using the labor, connection, wisdom and narratives of Black people to secure 'wins' that build their influence and power without simultaneously building the influence and power of Black communities who were supposed to benefit."

As a leader concerned about influence, I thought I might depersonalize the situation with Roberta and rally the board around this conversation, which could potentially spark dialogue throughout the nonprofit sector. I set up a meeting with the president of the local chapter of the Anti-Defamation League, an organization committed to stopping the defamation of Jewish people, hoping for support. A white Jewish colleague had suggested that the league could facilitate tough conversations between Black people and Jewish people. But about halfway through the conversation, he suggested that I focus more on Black and Jewish commonalities because "we struggled together during the civil rights movement."

My stomach tightened in response. My breathing became shallow, and my heart picked up its pace even as a squeezing sensation radiated from my chest. I calmly yet firmly pressed: "There is no way for our communities to have an authentic relationship if Jewish people cannot also acknowledge how our paths have diverged." His nonresponse told me we were at a stalemate. We both eased up and slid back into pleasantries about possibly working together. As I showed him the way out and the door closed with him on the other side, I shook my head. How convenient to suggest a focus on commonalities when all white people, including white Jewish people, came out on the upside of anti-Black racial oppression.

When David called me after Roberta's resignation, I offered (without being asked) to meet with her without a facilitator as she had requested if that would support her remaining on the board. I respected David and didn't want to disappoint him or anyone else. Amid the back-and-forth around this, Darakshan, a new board member, shared with me unprovoked that Roberta had made remarks in board meetings, one specifically about Muslim people, and she had wondered quietly, "I thought CHF was an antiracist organization."

At the outset of the meeting with Roberta, I had two things going for me: Darakshan's experience had affirmed my observations, and Avis had coached me on setting parameters for the meeting and taking notes. That advice grounded me and focused my attention so I could avoid getting sucked into Roberta's sunken place. After Roberta and I met one-on-one, I sent this detailed email to David and Roberta following the meeting.

> **From:** Yanique
> **Sent:** Wednesday, November 29, 2017
> **To:** David
> **Cc:** Roberta
> **Subject:** Recap of our conversation
>
> Dear David,
>
> Roberta opened by saying that she was appreciative of all I have done for the foundation. She then shared that she had been angry, upset and sad about the way things progressed and was very astonished especially after being the one who advocated for my bonus. She also stated that

she wondered if I was anti-Semitic. She then recounted the reasons why she resigned from the board and that the conversation with Avis made things worse for her.

I shared my profound disappointment that I asked for a facilitated conversation because I was not feeling safe and did not feel like the conversation would be productive, yet she resisted that for the last two months, even going above me to the board chair. I shared two of my ground rules for the conversation: 1) If I felt attacked in the conversation, I would end the conversation and 2) I would answer any of her questions but only once, given Roberta's history of asking me the same questions about this situation repeatedly. I asked Roberta if she had any ground rules that she would like to put on the table and she said she had none.

Roberta then asked two questions. What did I mean by "the Jewish response" in the last executive session and why couldn't we just sit down and talk about it?

I answered by providing a history of the critique of the Charlottesville statement that I authored for WRAG: We received a response from a Jewish member of the philanthropic community representing others from the Jewish community in philanthropy. I shared how devastated I was by that response given the content of the statement asking for a focus away from Charlottesville to the quiet forms of racism killing Black people every day. I shared that I should not have used the words "the Jewish response" because there is no one response from any group of people. However, there is clearly a Jewish response in the context of conversations about racism affecting people of color, which is "what about Jewish people?" I have experienced this response in multiple circumstances.

I then answered her second question. I shared that Roberta's response after the last board meeting (repeating three times to me "Jewish people are oppressed too" followed by an email sharing that anti-Semitic literature had been left on doorsteps in DC with the statement "It is not you but the environment") was my signal that this conversation was best had with a facilitator. There were three things at play: 1) my stress from a summer of resistance, racism and microaggressions, 2) her responses after the last board meeting and 3) the toxicity of the larger environment.

Roberta replied by saying that if I had told her this in a 10-minute conversation that this would have been done and that this is all she needed to hear. She said that it never had to get to this point and she was offended by the need for mediation.

I shared that I am looking forward to more board work on this because we can take leadership on this issue that is affecting several sectors in our community. I also think this board can do better in terms of how we have these tough conversations. I asked Roberta to let me know if she planned to stay on the board because we have meetings coming up and we weren't sure if we should send materials.

Roberta said she would remain on the board as long as she feels comfortable. She then described me as "aloof, formal, angry, guarded, demanding and not personal," and this didn't bode well for her staying on the board. She then wanted to know if we were going to be able to have a good relationship. I said we might be able to given the process that we will undertake as a board to learn how to have these tough conversations. Roberta then said she would be at the next board meeting and she would see where things go from there.

Yanique

Roberta resigned for the final time shortly after I sent this record. We haven't spoken since (except when I reached out to her to share excerpts from this book and to talk about our interactions, and she declined to read the excerpts, called me anti-Semitic, and blamed me for her departure from an organization she loved). I did not include my reactions in my email to David—how the reference she made to my bonus took my breath away in its seeming suggestion that she had power over my livelihood and that her power should buy my deference. Or how I might never fully recover from the slew of "angry Black woman" adjectives she flung at me during the meeting while I sat there and swallowed them. I wanted this record to speak for itself.

To this day, though I can't be completely sure, I don't believe I ever contracted Lyme disease. That fatigue? That feeling of wading through mud? The aches in my joints? They all pointed to the trauma common among Black leaders working in white spaces. That trauma had wormed its way into my body and made me sick. In *Weathering: The Extraordinary Stress of Ordinary Life in an Unjust Society*, Dr. Arline Geronimus recounts numerous studies that point to the "weathering" of marginalized peoples' bodies. The "weathering" hypothesis suggests that Black women's bodies break down faster than white women's bodies due to the weight of chronic racism-related stress. I can't help but wonder what irreparable damage has been done to my own heart and blood vessels over my life, including the years I endured the special brand of racism—the kind cloaked in good will—that we find in the philanthropic sector.

Though I really want it to, I don't suspect my class privilege will save me. Studies of birth outcomes among the richest Black women suggest that higher education and incomes don't completely shield us from racialized outcomes. For example, a study by the National Bureau of Economic Research found that babies born to the richest Black moms are still more likely to die within the first year of life compared to white babies born to the poorest white moms (Kennedy-Moulton et al. 2022). I don't have plans for more children. But I do have plans for a long life. I hope my heart can hold up.

To be fair, I believe Roberta had also been traumatized. The memory of her people's history likely haunted her in the context of rising incidences of anti-Semitism during Trump's presidency. She said as much: "It is not you but the environment." I did empathize with Roberta's Jewishness, and maybe if I had expressed that a bit more, she would have felt calmer, less threatened.

But Roberta was also white and had benefited from whiteness. When white Jewish people refuse to engage the white part of their identity, they run the risk of becoming a most troubling kind of racist. I'm not talking about the racists who storm capitols with the intent of overturning elections. Or the racists marching through the streets with guns. I'm talking about the allied racists, those who sit right next to us at decisionmaking tables, piping in to subtly block Black progress as they inflict the most egregious of harms—maintaining the status quo.

GUIDING QUESTIONS:

- How do you understand your and others' multiple identities? Which ones confer privilege? Which ones invite marginalization?
- What is your perspective on Black and Jewish solidarity? What is the opportunity for us to be in principled struggle?

10

MY BASEMENT

> It hurts like brand new shoes.
> —Sade, "Pearls," *Love Deluxe* album

My basement began flooding two days after Ronnie and I closed on our condo in one of the last wards in Washington, DC, where Black people still live. It was around the same time that I was becoming deeply deflated at work. I cried for hours on end for weeks as the unusually heavy rains caused water to seep from under the floor boards in the lower level. At least once a week, water flowed out of the basement bedroom into the hallway and traveled past the kitchen and into the living room, stopping short of the back door. Our new upstairs neighbor and only condo co-owner, Leah, a young white attorney, seemed concerned at first as we tried to work with the city to hold the two crooked developers accountable. But when the city left us hanging, we had no choice but to fix this $10,000 problem ourselves. At that point, Leah said the drainage system was not a condo association problem. We vehemently disagreed.

At the meeting with the closing agent for the seller to transfer ownership of the condo to me and Ronnie in unit one and Leah in unit two, we expected tension, but I could not have imagined the scenario that unfolded. Before Ronnie and I could even express our disapproval of Leah's stance on the drainage problem, she opened the meeting. With her hands outstretched toward us patronizingly, her palms facing downward, she attempted to calm us down. She said, "I know this is your first home."

I replied icily, "This is our third home," and watched the confusion on her face as she tried to backpedal.

She then rejoined, "My Realtor told me that this was your first home."

I angrily enunciated each word of my follow-up question: "Why are you and your Realtor talking about whether or not we are first-time homebuyers?" I continued, "And even if we are, why does that matter in the context of this drainage problem?"

She then retreated. "Well, I am a first-time homebuyer."

To which I replied through clenched teeth, "Well, talk about your damn self then!"

She began to cry and mumbled something about her grandfather's recent death and that she was taken aback by my hostility. Maybe the closing agent was affected by her tears; Ronnie and I certainly weren't. We just stared at her as she collected herself. As the oldest child of a woman who is often compared to the late Queen of England (a remnant of British colonization of Jamaica), I have learned how to be graceful and proper. I rarely let my anger erupt publicly. But my flooding basement had stripped me of all decorum in the face of this white woman's racist assumptions and attempts to weasel out of the condo association's responsibility. I was enraged.

During this period in my life, which I call the "meltdown," I phoned Ali, a good friend's sister who studies Egyptian spirituality. I don't remember why, but my friend had thought I might be interested in her sister's spiritual exploration. Ali told me about the dreams and visitations she had experienced and said that this ancient knowledge could set our people free. It was all very interesting and timely. I had been seeking alternatives to the crippling social justice work that consumed my every waking hour. As we were getting off the phone, she said, "My sister tells me that your basement is flooding."

With a sigh, I responded, "Yes," and told her that I had been weeping since it started, but I didn't quite know why. I had certainly had dark moments in my life where the tears made sense, but this situation didn't seem to rise to that level.

As casually as she had raised the subject, she replied, "It's perfectly understandable to me why this is happening. Your house represents you. The basement represents something unresolved in your subconscious. The flooding suggests you are overwhelmed by it." This couldn't be closer to the truth, and I knew instinctively what it was.

What remained unresolved for me was how my one little life could possibly be used as a tool to end the senseless suffering and death of Black people here in Washington, DC, and across America. This is what I fumbled to say to my therapist the day after talking to my Egyptian spirituality sage, and the tears welled up again. Seeing my despair, my wise therapist stepped out of therapy mode. "We're just going to talk as two professionals," she said.

"As a social worker who spent many years in DC, I have been where you are," she began. "I have seen landlords turn off the heat in buildings where poor Black people live to force them to leave so that they can flip the building and make money. When I drive by those buildings today, they have been turned into condos for white people. The policies that were put in place to displace poor Black people since Mayor Marion Barry's leadership are unfolding as they were designed, Yanique. If you are looking for transformative change, you are not going to find it in DC. Racism has been here and will continue to be here. Can you be satisfied with small changes?"

Her question broke my heart. I sobbed. I had been trying for so long to communicate that people are dying and they don't have to, but it seemed that people with power didn't care. It's as if there is a natural order and some people are disposable. I was devastated and forlorn. I was not and have never been satisfied with small changes. But in a strange way, as I walked out of my therapist's office, I found some comfort in her reminder of the long arc of history.

In the airport the day after, I picked up a book called *The Subtle Art of Not Giving a F*ck* by Mark Manson and downloaded it to my e-reader before getting on my flight. There were many things about this book that had me wondering why I paid $12.99 for it. But there were many things that were also right about this book, including the author's exposition at the end about immortality projects—projects that allow the conceptual self to live on way past the point of our physical death. It's our way of coming to terms with the perceived finality of death.

On that flight, I recognized that my pursuit of racial justice had been my immortality project. I didn't want my life to be for naught, so I had spent my entire career thus far working to prevent the death of Black people. Intellectually, I knew we all had to die, but why did so many of us have to die prematurely? And what was my role in stopping it? These two questions—these two questions alone—were *killing* me. This was my basement. And it was true that I had become overwhelmed by it. On top of the unwelcome water, mold crept farther up the walls each night, a constant reminder each morning of how much danger I was in. When I suggested to Ronnie that we walk away and foreclose on the condo, I was also channeling my resignation—I no longer had any fight.

In his book, Manson states that we ought to choose values that are simple, immediate, controllable, and tolerant of the chaotic world around us. My values were none of these. I want transformative change, and I want it now. However, to save myself, I needed to retool. I needed to declare a new set of values—ones that allow me to awaken each day, witness the devastation just blocks from where I live, play my part no matter how small, and believe it is enough. I decided that one small thing I could do was use words to articulate what I see and feel. Zora Neale Hurston has been quoted as saying, "If you are silent about your pain, they'll kill you and say you enjoyed it." If nothing else, I could use words as a record just in case others try to rewrite history, as has happened time and time again. Recall the narrative that enslaved Black people were happy and content? Someone had to say, "It ain't so." Thanks to Manson, I made a very simple promise to myself: I will write to record and expose. I took my first writing class at Politics and Prose Bookstore and began writing seriously. Not in defeat but in defiance, as my tears receded, my vision cleared, and my basement, while wet, no longer flooded.

GUIDING QUESTIONS:

- What is your immortality project?
- How do you come to terms with the possibility that certain changes may not happen in your lifetime?

11

A PLEASURE VIRGIN DISCOVERS THE ANTIDOTE TO WHITENESS

> i am certain that pleasure is the missing piece in our movement(s) for a new world.
> —adrienne maree brown, "the return of the pleasure activist"

AFTER ALMOST SIX YEARS IN THE PHILANTHROPIC SECTOR, I CLAWED my way out of a debilitating funk and found my therapist's couch ... again. I had tried on my own to deal with white women's microaggressions and backlash. I really had. Taking time off from work during a period of whiteness-induced fatigue. Studying with enthusiasm a convincing text on how to talk to white people about race. The book encourages the reader of color to be curious about white people's version of the truth, but I always felt like a fraud. I could hear myself asking white people, "Can you say more about that?" but I just didn't give a damn.

I sat on Dr. Brown's couch with my notebook and pen (because I am that girl), prepared to challenge my automatic thoughts born from old, recurring schemas. This bread and butter of cognitive behavioral therapy had saved me in the past. I had exorcised many a personal demon with CBT. Instead, she queried me about my "pleasure routine." Caught off guard by the question, I responded with a series of conflicting facial expressions—a blank stare, followed by a quizzical brow and then a slightly gaping mouth poised to reply. But I did not have a good answer, nor did I understand why, in the face of my dilemma with white women, this Black woman was asking me about pleasure.

I finally offered my love of travel. I do so with Ronnie a couple of times every year—the Caribbean mostly, but recently Paris and northern Spain. Unimpressed, she dug further for everyday pleasure, but I had nothing for her. I was not in a committed relationship with pleasure. Instead, I had been in a twisted ménage à trois of sorts with pain and suffering, and they were adamant about one thing: if it doesn't hurt, it's not worth doing.

Almost thirty years ago, when I met a troubled man who would become my first husband and then ex-husband shortly thereafter, I raised my hand eagerly for the job. "Yep, sounds like someone worth loving." Just a few years after that, a lesson in college about the US Public Health Service Syphilis Study at Tuskegee caused searing pain and uncontrollable run-out-of-the-classroom sobbing. What did I do? I applied to doctoral programs to research racism and health. "Yep, sounds like something to dig into."

The day after I defended my dissertation, I had coffee with a colleague, who asked how I had planned to celebrate. Celebrate? Didn't she know Black people were dying?

Dr. Brown assigned homework: "Pick one day each week and do something pleasurable."

"Like a project?"

"No," she replied. "I want you to do something with absolutely no goal. I want you to do something simply because it feels good."

I left bewildered and a touch woozy. At home I googled, "What do people do for pleasure?"

I opted to devote Sundays to pleasure and started with something easy: I indulged in a manicure and pedicure and then walked to a restaurant to eat brunch alone. The waitstaff tucked me away in a corner, where I enjoyed just one mimosa and an omelet. Sure, treating myself was cute, but I was certain this level of pleasure, as well as the standard recommendations to get massages, take walks, burn candles, and the like, would do nothing to extract me from the dark place I had found myself in.

The following Sunday, I scoped out movies online and went alone. It occurred to me as I entered the theater that I had never been to the movies by myself. How did I get to forty-two years old without the experience of negotiating with my own damn self about what I wanted to see? I saw a documentary, *Three Identical Strangers*, about triplets separated at birth who reunited randomly as young adults. I am attracted to stories about life's unpredictability. This suited me just fine. After the movie, I walked down by the Georgetown waterfront and watched people drinking and dancing on boats as the sun set. That seemed like fun. The longing for pleasure suddenly rising up in me.

As I made my way back to my car, I passed a sushi spot. I wanted to stop, but I kept walking. I have to get going, I thought. It's getting dark. Then I heard Dr. Brown: "Do something simply because it feels good." I didn't even have kids at home anymore. Why was I rushing home? I caught my reflection in the window of the restaurant as I made the U-turn. I sat by myself and enjoyed my favorite—shrimp nigiri. When I told Dr. Brown what I had done, she was so proud of me.

Dear reader, you must be wondering if this is real. It is. But I do graduate to far more interesting pleasures. Read on.

During my annual performance review in September, I risked telling my Board of Trustees that I felt exhausted from my constant interface with white people. I knew this diverse group of people thought highly of me, but it is difficult to tell your boss you are tired, no? Especially when your whole job involves meeting with and negotiating with said white people. I had also told them the same thing in my performance review the year before. I was sure my request for more time off would test their patience.

I revealed at the urging of my therapist (also hard to say) that I was seeking to discover pleasure and asked for two additional vacation weeks off around the Christmas holiday. Jackie, one of my biggest supporters on the board, asked quite unexpectedly, "Is there a reason you need to come back before the end of January?" They all nodded in agreement and approved a budget for mini-sabbatical expenses. This move by the board left me nonplussed. For most people, this counts as good news. For me, the luxury of seven weeks off spawned middle-of-the-night anxiety attacks accompanied by stern self-admonitions to get my act together. Leisure is for white women. Black women? We work. I eventually caved at Ronnie's urging and decided to study Spanish for four weeks in Mexico. This was the closest I was going to get to taking a break.

The holidays arrived three months after my performance review, and I flew home to Jamaica to celebrate my mom's seventieth birthday before leaving for Mexico. In Jamaica, I reveled in oxtails, curry goat, and escoveitch fish and found all kinds of pleasure in ackee and saltfish, fried dumplings and plantains. I danced and sang along with the steel band we had booked for the occasion as they played old folk songs—*dis lang time gyal mi neva see yuh, come mek me hol yuh han*—a glass of champagne lifted high above my head. That night, from the balcony of our house in the hills above Montego Bay, I burst with pleasure as I peered through my new oversize binoculars (purchased just because I thought they would please me) at the cruise ships leaving the port. I was certainly taking these on my pleasure journey!

Between my meeting with my board and my trip to Jamaica, I hired a personal trainer. To be clear, working out did not feel pleasurable. I despised all the ways my body lamented its soreness. I even tried to bribe my trainer: "Can I pay you more if we don't do that exercise again?" But I pressed forward. I needed to know if pleasure awaited me on the other side, and it did. My body grew stronger. Endorphins regularly flooded my brain, leaving me with that exercise high. And when people noticed my newly sculpted body and asked, "Are you working out?" that was pleasing to no end.

I spent the last four weeks of my mini-sabbatical studying Spanish each morning in Puerto Vallarta, Mexico, fulfilling a dream I'd had since I fell in love with the language in high school. I was in pleasure heaven. From time to time, Ronnie, who had not accompanied me, asked me about my plans after class. The answer was always the same: whatever pleases me. Most days I walked the five blocks to the beach and sat on the sand simply to feel the sun on my face. It's the part of my body that radiates intense feelings of pleasure when the sun's rays kiss it. And on the night of the blood moon, I climbed the stairs to the apartment rooftop and sat alone with my binoculars, caressed by the night sky and her moon, wide open to pleasure.

When I returned to work, I made no pretense about the threat that whiteness posed to my pleasure journey before I even had a chance to properly begin. To free up space and lighten my load, I resigned from everything I had been involved in, including two boards. I was a token on one and a witness to old-fashioned southern-inspired racism on the other. A case in point involved a fellow board member, who told us in her southern drawl that her spaces were so white, not even the servers at a function she attended recently were Black. This was the same board member who had protested the *Putting Racism on the Table* series during board conversations before its launch. She probably thought her admission demonstrated "wokeness." At least the white people around the table seemed uncomfortable, but no one said a word.

I regularly declined meeting requests if I didn't anticipate pleasure. People didn't like this, especially white people. A white colleague cornered me at an event and suggested we get together. She felt guilty about something she had said to me two years earlier. Two years! When I finished my post-mini-sabbatical-need-for-balance explanation as to why I could not meet, she quipped, "If we do something social, it won't be a meeting." I simply looked at her. I had no response.

At my office, I changed our dress code so that we could have the freedom to wear whatever we wanted as long as it was pleasing to the wearer. Most days you could find me in a graphic tee (like the one that read "Black Girl Magic") and skinny jeans or an African-print skirt. I could exhale after years of zipping myself into polished "professional" attire. I had wrongly assumed that my staple of long-sleeved blouses, J.Crew wool skirts, and pumps, along with my degrees, would make white people accept me and align with my antiracism cause. They didn't.

I am nowhere near to understanding the full spectrum of pleasure available to me. I am still a pleasure virgin who googles things like "What does it mean to have fun?" While doing so, I happened upon adrienne maree brown, author of *Pleasure Activism: The Politics of Feeling Good*. She is now my new shero, guide, and muse on the subject. A 2010 blog post about her pleasure principles (for example, "When I am happy, it is good for the world") provoked in me a visceral and fairly scary combination of rolling-on-the-floor laughter and streams of easy-flowing tears. She named what had been at the crux of my challenge all these years when she said pleasure "has become a politic for me … …living not just to the point of survival, but to the point of pleasure. i am certain that pleasure is the missing piece in our movement(s) for a new world."

I had been living to the point of my survival and the survival of others, Black people specifically. Even though I had been on a one-year pleasure journey, I still nursed a core belief that life was about pain, suffering, and survival. And in many ways, it is for Black people. But here was adrienne maree brown telling me that I could be Black *and* ascribe to pleasure and that pleasure could be a politic—an ideology, a worldview. These ideas were as foreign to me as Stevie Wonder's flying dolphins in his famous song "As," but they resonated as though I had always known them to be true.

Now, not every idea she proposes is for me. For example, she shares her own history of drug use as a path to pleasure (I have never even smoked a joint, people!), but so much in her book is exactly right for me: that I can "live to the point of pleasure." That pleasure is a "political activity, an act of resistance." That pleasure is a way to "reclaim my whole, happy, and satisfiable self from the impacts, delusions, and limitations of oppression and white supremacy." This is the journey I have now signed up for. And no matter what white women (or men) do or what pain and suffering have to say, there is no turning back. I cannot go back. This pleasure virgin has discovered that feeling good is the antidote to whiteness. And that, my friends, feels good.

GUIDING QUESTIONS:

- What does adrienne maree brown mean when she says pleasure has become a politic for her?
- What are your pleasure practices? Are any of them political?

12

NICKY

> White fragility functions as a form of bullying; I am going to make it so miserable for you to confront me—no matter how diplomatically you try to do so—that you will simply back off, give up, and never raise the issue again.
> —Robin DiAngelo, *White Fragility*

NICKY AND I SIT ACROSS FROM EACH OTHER IN A SMALL, LIGHT-FILLED breakfast spot in the heart of northwest DC. Her slimmed-down face has a pinkish glow to it, and there is levity behind her eyes. The last time we got together like this was for dinner about six months earlier. I let her know I was stepping down from my role of board chair of the Washington Regional Association of Grantmakers (WRAG) halfway through my two-year term. I was exhausted and needed distance from the sector, and the Consumer Health Foundation (CHF) board had offered me a mini-sabbatical as a reprieve. As a courtesy, I asked her if she would feel comfortable finishing out my term in her role as the board's vice chair. She said she was happy to do it but felt nervous.

She said she wanted to do right by my vision for internal racial equity. That is, hiring and staffing practices, supplier diversity, pay equity, and governance as distinct from the external *Putting Racism on the Table* series the association had launched three years back to nudge the sector toward racial equity.

The business part of our dinner, on that crisp fall evening, had taken all of thirty minutes. We spent the rest of the time, about two and a half hours, talking about life. My ex-husband had died by suicide a month before, leaving our young adult daughter both distraught and flattened, and I had just come back from a month in Atlanta with her as she buried him and tried to recover from the shock. I lamented about how awful it was to watch her suffer, knowing there was nothing I could do but sit and hold space with her as she cried. Nicky was raising two teenage sons, and my own stepson was in jail at twenty-one, which nearly destroyed me and was still eating away at Ronnie. We had been two mothers in that moment, and I left dinner feeling as if maybe we could move beyond being colleagues to friends.

Now, here we sit six months later, engaging in a full-on catch-up after ordering breakfast. "How was the mini-sabbatical?" she asks.

"Amazing." And I tell her all about the book *Pleasure Activism* and my efforts to simply feel good. "You look great," I add. "How are you doing?"

"I feel great. I have so much energy." Back and forth we go in easy conversation like two old friends.

The home she has bought is finally ready for guests, and she pauses ever so briefly before suggesting that Ronnie and I might spend the weekend. I am a tad uncomfortable. I like her. A lot. But that might be just beyond my comfort zone. She is white and trying, but she needs to do more work before I risk a weekend with her and the husbands. I avoid spending my precious weekend hours with white people. I don't want to edit myself or figure out how to react to a microaggression that is sure to come out of hiding and say *gotcha!* I lie and say, "Sure, that sounds great."

We return to our last conversation about the kids. My daughter is coping, but it's still rough going. Her sons are typical teenagers. We chat about WRAG, and we are both happy with the leadership transition between the beloved Tamara Copeland and the new unconventional leader Madye Henson. The fact that I left the board chair role suddenly is no longer news.

We pay for breakfast and begin reaching for our bags when Nicky sits forward and says, "Yanique, if there is something that I did to cause you to step back from philanthropy, please let me know." This surprises me. For some reason, I feel as though I have been ambushed. I cock my head to the left and look up and to the right. The pace of our chatty, high-speed conversation has suddenly shifted. The moment feels as if it is now unfolding in slow motion. My instinct is to say, "No, there is nothing," though I think to myself, Do I tell the truth?

"Well, actually, there is something," I venture.

I search her face as she eggs me on: "Please tell me."

"Remember the time I was trying to organize that panel conversation with Ari Theresa on gentrification in DC?"

She nods yes as she sits back in her seat.

"Well, when you said that you couldn't participate because your board would not go for it, that's when I realized that allies like you in organizations like Meyer would only go so far. I know you have to deal with your board, so I don't blame you for it. But that realization was hard for me. It was part of the exhaustion."

She quietly folds her arms. That healthy flush on her face dissipates, and her skin now has a yellowish cast. Her eyebrows knit in a growing scowl. "You must have been mistaken," she spits.

I had been warned by a colleague that Nicky had a single objective, and that was to carry on the legacy of her predecessor, Julie Rogers, who had reigned over DC philanthropy for twenty-eight years. The *Washington Business Journal* had said of Julie when she stepped down in 2013, "Julie is the rare leader in Washington. She is the ultimate straddler. While she is firmly rooted in the nonprofit community, she straddles the sectors. Business and government leaders turn to her for advice and counsel" (Orfinger 2013). The *Washington Post* said she "is credited with helping to shape Washington's philanthropic community. Under her tenure, the Meyer Foundation's assets rose from $50 million in 1986 to $210 million this year" (Brown 2013). The *Washingtonian* magazine named Julie one of the region's "100 Most Powerful Women" in 2011, the same year that Nicky was also bestowed with the title (Milk 2011). At the time, Nicky was head of the Washington Area Women's Foundation.

From my perspective, old DC philanthropy was devoid of racial equity and justice. It seemed to heavily emphasize charity—giving away money to *help* the needy—at the expense of transformative systems change that would *eliminate* need altogether. This kind of charity-based philanthropy built careers and compensated well but never allowed poor people of color a seat at its tables. This kind of philanthropy negotiated with the power brokers to keep back-breaking, soul-killing systems in place, while using its reputation of giving away money to help those less fortunate to obscure its trade-offs. I didn't see Nicky as advocating for this kind of philanthropy. Yes, she kept company with the power brokers as Julie had, but unlike Julie, she led with racism. It's the reason I had experimented with being in an intimate space with her. As a matter of pragmatism, I also needed this white woman to publicly validate what I had been saying all along—the root of the challenges in communities of color is racism.

From the outside, Nicky was checking all the right racial equity boxes. Within a year of taking the helm at Meyer, she had instituted an equitable hiring process and made it clear to the search firm that she wanted the candidate pool to be diverse and include people from a variety of backgrounds who had experience with racial equity. She had the firm remove the markers of race from résumés so that applicants' skills and experiences for top leadership positions—vice president of programs, director of equity and strategy, director of DC partnerships, and director of Virginia partnerships—could be analyzed objectively. That search led to the hiring of Black women for three out of the four positions.

Nicky had also recruited two new Black board members to the Meyer board and had involved white board members in *Putting Racism on the Table*. One prominent white businessman and Meyer board member had attended the series and seen the light. He began positioning himself to spread what he had learned throughout the business sector (as an aside, the business sector has not done anything consequential regarding racial equity in the DC region).

Nicky and I were also collaborating on DC in Color, a partnership with the Urban Institute to quantify what would have to change in people's lives—education, income, assets—for DC to become an equitable city. When I had pitched the project to Nicky, she admitted that Meyer did not yet have the programmatic expertise around racial equity, so she was excited to partner, learn, and grow. We were also on the speaking circuit together. I would share ideas on the leading edge of racial equity at a progressive foundation, and Nicky would share her perspective as a newbie turning a ship. I used these examples to vouch for her, but my colleague would not relent: Nicky was using race—the topic du jour—to increase her visibility and gobble up airtime. But I just didn't see it that way.

Nicky and I met up at Tabard Inn for a similar breakfast meeting a couple of years back. She needed an ear as she waded deeper into tricky waters with a mostly white board representing the Washington elite. She felt that some of her board members were not pleased with her moves to transform Meyer into a more equitable institution. I had never seen her so rattled. Compared with Julie's leadership, Nicky's looked qualitatively different—justice-driven and vulnerable.

Don't get me wrong; I am not applauding her. Too many Black women's careers have been derailed because they speak up for Black people (exhibit A: Nikole Hannah-Jones as she fought for tenure at University of North Carolina), so Nicky won't get a pat on the back from me. But going against the grain to advance racial equity and getting heat for it was a demonstration of her commitment. This was the sacrifice I had hoped to see from my white peers. Are you willing to lose something—anything—in support of justice?

"Don't get too close to Nicky," my colleague had warned. But I had ignored the warning until now. The scowl on her face reminds me that maintaining white privilege will always be more important than Black people's truth. Seeing what appeared to be defiance on her face and in her body language, I feign the possibility that I might have gotten events mixed up. She says she doesn't recall backing out of the gentrification event. I tell her I will go back through my emails when I get to the office and forward to her what I find. We part ways. My ability to racial cape—to calm white people down—allows us to leave amicably. But as I get farther from the restaurant, my anger builds. By the time I step into my office, I am furious.

I throw my bag on the floor and plop down in my chair. Why did she ask for feedback if she was going to defend herself? I shake my mouse vigorously to restart my computer, click on the Trash icon in my email inbox, and search for emails from Nicky in 2018. I continue to berate myself: "Why did I put myself out there?" I find the email I am looking for. In response to my request for Meyer to cohost the gentrification event, she had said, "I am interested but this is an area where I get strong pushback from the developer members of my board. This was basically the conversation we had after the Richard Rothstein event."

Richard Rothstein, the white author of *The Color of Law: A Forgotten History of How Our Government Segregated America*, had apparently spooked the real estate developers on the Meyer board. A distinguished fellow at the Economic Policy Institute, Rothstein had spoken twice to the philanthropic community about the country's legacy of housing discrimination and neighborhood segregation and its lasting impacts on the racial wealth gap. I was at both of his talks, and two things struck me (beyond the shameful pushback from two white men in the audience at his second talk): Rothstein said he was an education researcher, not a housing and neighborhood researcher. However, he ended up studying racial residential segregation because he kept bumping into it as he worked to grasp the root causes of education inequities.

Schools in middle- and upper-middle-class white neighborhoods had more resources because school-funding formulas are based on taxes paid by homeowners. Redlining in the 1950s—a federal government–driven process to determine mortgage risk by rating neighborhoods based on several factors, including the race of the people living there—had denied homeownership to generations of African Americans, leaving Black schools underfunded. He also suggested reparations as a solution without using the term. During one of his talks, he shrugged his shoulders casually and asked, "What if African Americans could purchase homes at greatly reduced prices?"

I stare at my email inbox and start to craft a response to Nicky, but I need to talk to someone about my anger. I get up from my desk and walk around the office suite, assembling the staff. We all convene in Ria's office. I ask out loud what I had been thinking all the way back from breakfast: "Why did Nicky ask for feedback if she was going to defend herself?" Ria shakes her head and utters, "Tsk, tsk, tsk." We agree that this is white fragility in action. I ask them for advice. "Should I follow up? What if we lose Meyer's partnership?" They all agree that I need to voice my disappointment. I walk back to my office and construct this email to Nicky, an email I would not have penned prior to my mini-sabbatical:

From: Yanique
Sent: Wednesday, June 26, 2019
To: Nicky
Subject: FW: Have you seen this?

Hey Nicky, great to catch up. It was the event related to Ari Theresa talking about zoning policies and how they impact gentrification in the city. See below. It was in response to my invitation to you to co-host this event that you said your board members would push back. Eventually, Urban Institute and Brookings said the same thing and the event fell apart. If you read Ari's case against the District, it is one of the clearest statements for equity that I have seen, but no one would participate.

Like I said then and today, I get the challenges that you have with your board. But ultimately, I left that situation and many others that I have encountered with the feeling that things may not change. We are all protecting our personal and institutional self-interests.

On another topic (and we can talk later): you asked me to provide feedback about your possible role in my recent disappointments in philanthropy and decision to pull back. I shared the above situation with you, and your first response was that I misunderstood. I acknowledge that I was unclear about which request I had made (I knew it was either this one or the What Happened 2 Chocolate City one), but I knew that you declined for the reason you stated below.

Frankly, because of how closely I live these issues, I rarely misunderstand. But I can't tell you how often white people tell me that I have misunderstood or that something they did say was not said when confronted with personal accountability around race issues. I don't have enough fingers to count the times! So, I am often left doubting myself. Did I mishear? Did I misinterpret? Did I misread? Even when I know I didn't.

I am not sure what your intention was, but I thought I would share the impact. You asked for the feedback. I took the risk to share. And your response was impactful. I should have said so in the moment, but as usual, I am shocked when these kinds of things happen, and I don't know how to respond.

Yanique

She replies a couple of hours later to say that she didn't intend the impact and that "we/Meyer were not in a place to take a public facing role and position with the panel at that time." She continues, "I understand your frustration about that. It will take us a couple of iterations of our board to get to that next place, and I was/am constantly picking my battles. Someone described it to me when I explained our evolution as organizing the board towards our common purpose—I feel like that's a good way to look at it."

Her email response does not feel right to me. It is missing something, but I can't quite pinpoint what it is. I had said at breakfast that I understood the position she was in with her board and didn't blame her for my frustration with the sector. At around 10 p.m., she sends this follow-up email:

From: Nicky
Sent: Wednesday, June 26, 2019
To: Yanique
Subject: FW: Have you seen this?

And upon further reflection, I also apologize for the defensiveness of my response this morning. Heading out tomorrow - will connect when I'm back. Nicky

This is what is missing—an apology regarding her angry response to my feedback at *her* request. Though at this point, her apology means nothing. She addressed the most painful part of our interchange footnote style.

* * *

I LOOK DOWN at my phone during a CHF staff meeting and see a strange email from Terri, the vice president of programs at Meyer. I had been in the same circles with Terri for years; we matriculated from the same institution with PhDs in public health but at different times. She says she is in agony and needs to enlist my support. After the staff meeting, I head to the privacy room to take her call. Terri is bawling. I can't even understand what she is saying. I try to calm her down, but it's not working. I make out that she has been fired after twenty months at Meyer and she doesn't know why. She has been given a week to sign an agreement outlining her severance pay and is expected to refrain from disparaging the foundation upon signing it.

Beyond the *why* of her firing, she is devastated about the *how*. She tells me that she was summoned to Nicky's office, and when she walked in, Nicky and Meyer's HR consultant were waiting. She says she had no frame of reference for the scene unfolding in front of her. She says they explained that she was being let go, and the HR consultant followed her to her office to pick up her purse and briefcase before escorting her out and taking her keycard and file cabinet key. She was then escorted to her vehicle and told that she could come back after hours, on the weekend or the upcoming holiday to gather her items. "As if I stole something!" she wails. I am an empath and feel this in my belly. I just keep saying, "I'm so sorry, Terri," and reassure her that she can call me again if she needs to process it further. I tell her that in our staff meeting, Ria and Kendra had just voiced their gratitude for her partnership on the effort by funders to increase the census count in the region. I want her to know that we value her even if Meyer doesn't.

I didn't know Terri well, but I knew her well enough to know that another way was possible. Top executives in philanthropy get let go sometimes. It happens. But could Nicky not have found another way to let her Black vice president go, especially after being so determined to create an equitable hiring process? No transition consultancy? Or going-away party? I plan to call Nicky to say just this, but I am so angry, I can't bring myself to dial her number.

The following week, Nicky beats me to it and calls. She is making the rounds to tell partners that Terri is gone. But she can't disclose much. "It's confidential," she says. I tell her that this feels sudden. She says it isn't and casually asks how my kids are doing. I tell her that I have to go and will talk to her later. I think to myself, I cannot have this conversation with you right now.

* * *

THERE IS a buzz in the air. WRAG is hosting its 2019 annual meeting. It is Madye Henson's first meeting as the new president, and Edgar Villanueva, author of *Decolonizing Wealth*, is the keynote speaker. There is also another first. CHF has invited community members with recent lived experience of poverty and class oppression to the meeting. We purchased twenty-four seats to accommodate thirteen community members who are attending with CHF board and staff. In the mix are two Spanish-language interpreters for Dilcia, a new member of the CHF board who primarily speaks in Spanish. A few weeks earlier, when Dilcia attended a WRAG event for CEOs and trustees with an interpreter, people kept turning their heads and staring to find out where the whisper was coming from. Gretchen, the association vice president, had expressed her disappointment that we hadn't given them a heads-up; they wanted to prevent that "disruption" from happening again, this time at their signature event.

The ballroom continues to hum as guests stream in and network. Along with the other CHF staff, I greet each community member, sometimes stooping in between chairs to say hello and answer questions. Once in a while, someone from another foundation comes over to our table to greet us. If I am with a community member, I am sure to make an introduction. As I am talking with one such person, I catch Nicky out of the corner of my eye. She is waiting to speak to me. When the conversation wraps up, Nicky approaches me. She has a desperate look on her face. She begins crying.

"Yanique, I am so sorry," she begins.

"Why are you sorry?" I respond quizzically, even though I know what's behind the tears. I had been distant since our breakfast and even more so since her firing of Terri the month before.

"I just don't want you to write me off," she begs.

"Nicky, I am not writing you off," I say as I reach out to touch her arm comfortingly. I struggle to know what to do. I am shocked at this display of what I would call white fragility. Nicky had participated in several racial equity trainings, including one led by

Robin DiAngelo, who literally wrote the book *White Fragility*. In my opinion, Nicky should know that white women's tears are egregious. She should know that her tears center white women's experiences and overshadow the experiences of people of color. She should know that white women's tears have been weaponized to threaten people of color and sidestep accountability. She should know that white women's fragility has gotten Black people killed.

"Let's talk some more," I say. It's my way of ending this awkward moment, not only because of the poor timing of this scene but also because this powerful white woman is weeping openly in front of a room full of people gathering for a meeting, and she needs to pull herself together.

She nods in response to my suggestion that we talk, and as she turns away, she begs again, "Please don't write me off."

* * *

A YEAR LATER, Terri still doesn't have a job. She is late on her mortgage, but luckily, due to COVID, she is in a program to delay penalties and negative reporting to credit bureaus. She decides to move away from DC because she feels "untouchable," though she says this experience offered her an unencumbered opportunity to contemplate a different future.

* * *

IN THE SPRING OF 2021, Nicky calls to tell me that she is stepping down as president of the Meyer Foundation. I know that's why she is calling because word is already getting around. I don't answer the phone. I still don't know what to say to her. A little over a year earlier, we met for coffee a few weeks after the tear-filled scene at the WRAG annual meeting. She still couldn't say much about Terri's firing, only that it hadn't been working out. Someone on the

Meyer staff told me that Terri wasn't jibing with the team. But I was very frank with Nicky: There was another way to coach Terri if that was the only issue. And even if you had to let her go, you could have done so in a way that preserved her dignity and prospects for future employment.

Since that conversation, Madye filed a wrongful termination suit against WRAG and Nicky in her role as WRAG's board chair. I was done. "Who is next?" I asked when I got the call from an association board member telling me that Madye was no longer the president. "Tonia?" Tonia was the new Black president of the Greater Washington Community Foundation. Nicky, who represented her foundation and its donation to the Community Foundation's COVID Fund, had been urging Tonia to apply racial equity criteria to the fund's grantmaking protocol. Though I agreed with Nicky's rationale—she and her coconspirator Hanh wanted to see more resources going to POC-led nonprofits—I wished she would tread lightly. I could almost hear the death knell summoning the end of Tonia's community foundation career if she took the risk and championed racial equity as a new leader in white spaces, leading to the biggest exodus of fund holders from the foundation. Charles Schwab and Fidelity would be happy to take wealthy white people's moneys and not hold them accountable to any racial equity goals. I was nervous for Tonia after what had happened to Terri and Madye.

But Madye fought back. On June 30, 2020, Madye filed a lawsuit against WRAG, Nicky, and others on the WRAG board and staff. She retained the New York–based Cochran Firm, founded by the legendary Johnnie Cochran, who used the famous words "If it doesn't fit, you must acquit" to get O. J. Simpson acquitted of murder charges. In the lawsuit, Madye alleged that WRAG "has done little to address its own internal race issues," even as the association trained its members to consider systemic racism. The lawsuit also pointed to Nicky's firing of Terri as evidence of her "history of dismissing leaders of color" and said that "Dr. Henson was next on Defendant Goren's target list." My sudden departure as chair of the WRAG board showed up in the lawsuit as a red flag. Madye said she had asked to speak to me during the interview process, but Nicky denied her the opportunity. I had been unaware of this until I read the thirty-nine-page lawsuit, which unfolded like a 1980s soap opera. Maybe that's what made the Cochran Firm so good: they know how to tell a good story.

My reaction to the lawsuit was mixed. There was glee. Finally, someone had taken on the racism running rampant in the sector. *The Exit Interview: Perceptions on Why Black Professionals Leave Grantmaking Institutions*, a 2014 report by LM Strategies for the Association of Black Foundation Executives, calls out the high churn rate of Black people in the philanthropic sector. Even though these are high-status, good-paying jobs with benefits, where one can stay a lifetime if one chooses, Black people were leaving because of burnout from daily microaggressions and blatant discrimination.

We also leave because we come to the sector to work on behalf of our communities, believing we can create change by giving money away. Then we inevitably realize that change is not the objective in philanthropy. The objective is largely to make things manageable enough for people experiencing various forms of oppression. Even for those foundations with higher aspirations, boards of mostly white trustees don't allow us and those living on the edge to have any real say. They believe they know best. Anyone who braves the potential backlash and takes on this system is my shero.

At the same time, I had serious misgivings about Madye. The first time we met one-on-one after she was hired, she said a most peculiar thing—that the business sector had been a leader in racial equity for decades. In the few conversations I had with her, mainly in passing, she never asked for my opinion on furthering the association's racial equity work. She seemed to have her sights set on the business sector and growing its involvement in WRAG as the main feature of her revenue strategy. She had sold herself in the interview as a racial equity leader, and I had given her my vote, but she came across as anything but that. What had I done?

Madye had successfully run a large social service nonprofit focused on youth who are homeless, and I was excited to see someone from the nonprofit sector who had worked directly with poor folks apply for the position. She didn't come across as knowing the racial equity scholarship and terminology, but I thought she had natural instincts. Her story about creating special educational opportunities for Black kids who were failing inside of the Alexandria city public school system sealed it for me during the interview. I thought she could learn the language and scholarship of racial equity along the way. I also loved that she was not respectable in the way that some Black people work hard to be in white spaces. She gave it to you straight, no chaser. But after just a month, I realized I had made a mistake in joining others on the Hiring Committee to recommend her for the role of WRAG president.

In addition to stating in the lawsuit that my sudden departure had been a red flag, she divulged her conversations with Nia (who worked for WRAG before joining CHF) and Kendra (who worked at WRAG on a special project while working at CHF). They had both shared with Madye their experiences of the hostile work environment at WRAG so that she might intervene to make the organization wholly aligned with its public persona as a racial equity leader. Madye included all this in the lawsuit but never spoke directly to me, Nia, or Kendra. This felt opportunistic. I grew suspicious of her motives. Her lawsuit did not feel like an effort to "change the leadership and culture of WRAG." I didn't believe Madye cared about any of us. Still, something needed to be done, and Madye did it. Terri followed suit and filed her own action against the Meyer Foundation and Nicky less than a month later. If I must choose sides, I will choose Madye and Terri every time.

Nicky is stepping down amid this backdrop, yet in her public announcement, she says that "a critical aspect of leadership is knowing when to make space and pass the baton." She says nothing about her embattled leadership, only that she will serve as a senior advisor to the foundation and will write a book about Meyer's—and her own—racial equity journey. That's what you call a soft landing! Neither Terri nor Madye—both highly qualified, pedigreed leaders—got that opportunity to leave their organizations with such a perfectly curated narrative.

Though Nicky was dismissed from the WRAG lawsuit, the association settled with Madye for an undisclosed amount in the summer of 2021, and even though I have my misgivings, I hope she walked away with a boatload of money. At the time of this writing, a judge dismissed Terri's action against the Meyer Foundation following the foundation's motion to dismiss, and Terri has since appealed and is waiting on a favorable outcome.

Following the WRAG settlement, the *Washington Post*, whose money created the Meyer Foundation's endowment, published an exposé detailing the two lawsuits in an article titled "A Racial Reckoning at Nonprofits: Black Women Demand Better Pay, Opportunities" (Trent 2021). Thus Nicky didn't get the final say. Everyone who read the article now has another perspective on what transpired behind closed doors, even though Meyer's board chair, a Black woman, was quoted in the article as saying that the allegations have no merit. If Meyer and WRAG would just admit where they erred, even if it means a financial and reputational cost to the institutions, they would do more to advance racial equity than with any of their programmatic efforts. In my opinion, denying these two Black women's experiences reinforces the very systems they say they are attempting to change. The legal system says, "Defend, defend, defend." Racial equity demands admission and reparation.

The *Washington Post* article got a few things right. It cited a study from the Building Movement Project in which Black women talked about their experience in the sector with "lower pay, being overlooked for jobs and promotions, lack of mentorship, dealing with assumptions that they are underqualified and being stereotyped as 'angry Black women.'" Resourcing Radical Justice (RRJ), a funder collective I cofounded with Rubie Coles of the Diverse City Fund at the top of the COVID-19 pandemic, did its own survey of people of color in the local philanthropic sector, and we heard similar stories.

Rubie and I founded RRJ to rally aligned funders around getting resources to nonprofits led by Black people and people of color that had small budgets and were working on both systems change and direct service delivery in response to COVID-19. However, we had a secondary motive: we needed our own space in philanthropy to do this work beyond the white gaze and in response to our own knowledge of what was needed. For example, most of the moneys that were being collected for COVID-19 relief —much of it going to the Greater Washington Community Foundation—were being directed toward the larger nonprofits, many of which were white-led and had little interest in radically shifting our systems so that it would be impossible for someone like Amazon's Bezos to see his net worth explode during the pandemic while many of our poorest residents, almost all people of color, couldn't pay rent or buy diapers. In addition to the advocacy that Nicky and Hanh were leading from the inside, RRJ tried to influence the Community Foundation to direct some of its resources differently through our relationship with its new Black leader. In the midst of our efforts to steer the resources we controlled and do what we could to move others' money, RRJ members discovered a safe space of healing with each other. The survey idea came out of a desire to find out how our peers of color were coping.

Analogous to the study findings quoted in the *Washington Post* article, our peers talked about watching white employees do mediocre work and get rewarded time and time again in the normal course of business, while they remained underpaid, overworked, and actively excluded from advancement opportunities. They shared stories of cringeworthy anti-Blackness, including one in which a wealthy white man and donor said about the DC government's Black women in leadership, "I am not racist, but that's some Black pussy power right there." I sat on my bed on a Sunday afternoon reading the results, hot tears streaming down my face. It was the first time I shed tears about work since I had withdrawn from actively participating in sector convenings to focus on myself and my institution. I had only returned to external-facing meetings because of the safety of RRJ and in response to the COVID-19 crisis. But here I was again butting up against the sector's cruelty. I was certainly not surprised by the survey results, but reading the concrete examples of racism and discrimination in people's own words brought back memories and heartache that remained right below the surface.

The article got another thing right. The author said, "The experiences of Black women within nonprofits are similar to those at for-profit companies, except for one noteworthy difference: Nonprofit leaders and board members—the overwhelmingly majority of whom are White—often perceive themselves as society's do-gooders" (Trent 2021). While many corporations pay extraordinary sums to present an image that will outshine practices that hurt the environment, abuse workers, and amass profits, philanthropic organizations can cause similar harm with few to no consequences. In our sector, we can quietly marginalize our workers of color, invest our endowments in companies that gentrify neighborhoods or imprison Black and Brown people, and schmooze with the elites of any city or town. But we have a built-in Olivia Pope—simply the fact that we give money away.

Although the *Washington Post* article got two things right, it also got two things wrong. It wrapped the story around Nicky, who was just an easy target within a sector that is deeply and possibly irreparably flawed. Newsrooms need personal stories, so I get that. But, in my opinion, Nicky is just one of many white women in the sector who are like elephants in a porcelain shop. Some knowingly and others unknowingly wield their power recklessly. Instead of going out of their way to support Black leadership, they take up too much space and undermine our efforts.

The way I see it, these white women are just too ambitious with their racial equity agenda. Especially those who are early in their personal journeys. With few exceptions, this can be said of almost all white women in DC-area philanthropy (and probably in philanthropic institutions across the country). In addition, let's not forget the role of board members, to whom CEOs are accountable. In our sector, boards of trustees almost always trail the staff when it comes to racial equity and justice. Let's not forget the role of boards of trustees who wield power but are never seen.

The article also conflated philanthropy with the larger nonprofit sector of which foundations are a part. While nonprofits struggle with the same issues, the philanthropic sector is its own beast and deserves its own calling out distinct from the problems plaguing the charities that seek money from the sector every day. Nonprofit organizations may be overseers, but the philanthropic sector is the colonizer. We need to isolate the sector and its oppressive practices so we can see it for what it is.

GUIDING QUESTIONS:

- How have you experienced white women's tears being used to distract from issues of racism and discrimination?
- Beyond tears, what other strategies have white women used to maintain power?

PART III
US

13

HOW DOES IT FEEL TO BE A COMPROMISE?

> To the real question, How does it feel to be a problem? I answer seldom a word.
> —W. E. B. Dubois, *The Souls of Black Folk*

I WISH DARAKSHAN, SILVIA, AND WENDY WERE BLACK. OR AT LEAST one of them were Black. They joined the Consumer Health Foundation (CHF) board between 2014 and 2016, when we were seeking organizers, activists, and advocates who were in deep relationship with communities hit especially hard by racial capitalism, but none of the three were building primarily with slave-descended African Americans. Asian, yes. Non-Black Latino, yes. Even Black immigrants. But certainly not Black DC natives. The fact that none of the three are Black makes me sad. For goodness' sake, this is Chocolate City, with its history of both leadership by and oppression of Black people, and not one of the three lives in a Black body? I am afraid that this line of questioning otherizes or diminishes them, but I have to ask myself if anti-Blackness was at play in our recruitment process. I am sitting with my own role in this turn of events. We are here now.

I brought Darakshan, Silvia, and Wendy together for two Zoom conversations between November 2020 and January 2021 to better understand their experiences as the transition trustees between the board of the past, whose members all had degrees and middle-class sensibilities, and the board of the future, grounded in the lived reality of people who currently struggle the most in our region. Both conversations occurred after the 2020 election amid the national anxiety surrounding the drawn-out electoral vote tally followed by the January 6, 2021, storming of the US Capitol.

Knowing that what I really wanted to talk about was sensitive, I asked a warm-up question in the first conversation: "In what season do you find yourself and CHF both personally and professionally?" Darakshan, who was off video, spoke to the national climate, "It feels like fall going into winter in terms of COVID and the coup we are in right now. It just feels like such a daunting moment."

I had known them all for some time, but I didn't want to make assumptions about their identities. I asked, "How do you identify racially, ethnically, and in other ways that are important in terms of how you want the world to see you or how you believe the world sees you?" They all wanted me to know that while they were recruited for one part of their identity—proximity to poor people of color—they are much more than that.

Wendy, who is in her forties, identified herself as a queer woman of color who is white passing and perfectly middle-class. She acknowledged her education and how it afforded her the privilege she has today. She was born in Hawaii and grew up there, but she is not native Hawaiian because her family is Chinese. And as fifth-generation Chinese in Hawaii, she does not see herself as a new immigrant. She is also half white and shared that being white is an "absolute outsider" identity in Hawaii. Moreover, there was something about her identity that she felt but couldn't quite explain in words. When she tried, it came out as growing up in a "mixed-race colonial and monarchy situation." She explained, "It has been a feeling that I have never really talked about. It's not a mainland experience. It's something, but I can't quite articulate it." She made it clear that she was a "paid advocate," not someone who struggles on the margins.

Silvia, who is in her thirties, described herself as bicultural and bilingual. She is both Latina and indigenous, though she does not know which indigenous tribe she is from—a product of colonization in central America. A key part of her identity is that she grew up undocumented and watched her mom negotiate whiteness. Silvia's mom, a housekeeper, interacted carefully with her employer to keep the woman happy and in doing so kept their prospects for a green card alive. Silvia is now a citizen, but fear of deportation is still central to who she is and how she sees the world. She added that she is deaf in one ear and a brain tumor survivor, which explains her identity as a person with a disability. Even on this call she was wearing sunglasses because a recent accident had left her with light sensitivity, compounded by the previous brain tumor.

I had visited Silvia during her recovery from the accident to bring her a gift and once again to meet about our community-based transformation, so I knew exactly where she was sitting while on the Zoom call. The brick-red wall in her background was right at the entrance of the small one-bedroom unit she was sharing temporarily with her mother, who had come from Los Angeles to take care of Silvia and had to stay due to COVID. Silvia was now mostly recovered and back to work, where she contributed to studies in and with Native American communities at a federal agency. But in her spare time, she was an organizer who lived in a building she and her neighbors had bought to create an affordable housing cooperative.

Darakshan is not yet thirty-five and is both Pakistani and American. When asked about her identity, she paused and then said she has layers of identities within each of her core identities. In America, she identifies as a South Asian Pakistani American immigrant within the diaspora who identifies both politically and religiously as Muslim. Within her Pakistani identity, she is both Punjabi and Pashtun, which are tribal identities. She also considers herself a brown woman of color. She is from an immigrant working-class family in New York City, which she said is its own identity. She is an activist and nonprofit leader who organizes Muslim women, and she is a grantee partner of the foundation.

In the second interview, when I asked a warm-up question about what we were all celebrating, Darakshan shared that she had finally made space in her life for her hobby as a DJ. Silvia had taken up knitting. Wendy's job situation was changing. It was going to be big and she couldn't yet say.

As I document their identities, I am aware that racial capitalism[1]—defined by University of Denver professor Nancy Leong as the process of extracting social and economic value from a person of a different racial identity (referring predominantly to the extraction of value from those of nonwhite identity)—wants nothing to do with these complex identities. It prefers to flatten us and categorize us so that we can be placed in the hierarchy of human value. This reminds me of a germane passage from Edgar Villanueva's *Decolonizing Wealth*: "In their intoxicated rush to consolidate wealth, colonizers reduced the number of religions, languages, species, cultures, social systems, media channels, and political systems. On all scales, global to local, this homogenizing campaign—*global bleaching*, you could call it—made the world not just more bland and boring but also less innovative and resilient." (2018, 63).

At various points in the conversation, each talked about the interview process they went through to join the board. Wendy recalled using the word *justice* in her interview. She thought, "Oh shit, I blew that." She sensed that the foundation did not yet use this word. "That was too far." She also felt intimidated. "Everybody had a PhD," she said. "I felt like a double impostor. In one sense, the board's description of community was not me. I am in relationship with and my values are aligned with community members who have lived experience of poverty, but I am not someone who has personal experience with poverty. On the other end, this was an esteemed, distinguished, professional, and super-qualified table, and everyone had degrees." This did not feel like her identity either. It wasn't until much later, when Kendra, CHF's program associate, invited a conversation about gender and LGBTQ identity at one of our board and staff retreats, that Wendy felt permission to express her own personal experience. Wendy might not have experienced poverty, but she did have the experience of being queer, and LGBTQ identity also mattered for people of color. "I hate myself" for not speaking up, she said. "Why couldn't I say that this work is also about LGBTQ identity for people of color?"

This powerful woman of color, who ran campaigns to advance paid sick leave policy in her day job and now runs a federal agency bureau, felt like an impostor when interviewing to be on the Consumer Health Foundation board. If she felt that way on the board of what I call a "very small edgy foundation" that doesn't follow the conventions of philanthropy, what must it feel like to be a community member with lived experience of poverty in these spaces? And what will it take to decolonize much larger foundations like the Gates Foundation, the Robert Wood Johnson Foundation, and the Annie E. Casey Foundation?

Silvia also shared her own experience of loneliness and anxiety when she joined the board. She had been the first of the three recruited. "Everybody was more accomplished than me," she said. "They understood finances. Everybody dressed so nicely. I felt I had to up my game. For the first year, I held my breath and metered myself in terms of what to say. I presented issues in the least offensive way possible because I wasn't sure about how far I could go. When Darakshan and Wendy joined, I felt like I could take more risk."

At the same time, when in community spaces, Silvia felt guilty about her position of power and downplayed being a trustee, a sentiment that Darakshan echoed. Silvia was also deeply troubled by Roberta, a white trustee on the board. She had once greeted Roberta at the airport, but she said Roberta looked right through her, rendering her invisible. She recalled the liturgical dance performance set to my and others' perspectives on racism, recorded at a philanthropy meeting, and Roberta's dismissive response to it when the board watched it together. She pointed as well to Roberta's anti-Black tropes about crime.

Darakshan confessed that she had not thought she would get selected to be on the board. She shared, to much laughter, her cavalier approach to the interview as the codirector of a "dingy small organization." She told us how she hesitated to submit her application to join the board even though Ria, the foundation's senior program officer, had encouraged her to apply. She had asked herself, What could they possibly want from me? For a while after joining the board, she often wondered, Do I even belong? Have I accomplished enough to sit at the table? Have I earned the right to be in this space? "Some of this is white supremacy," she said, "but some is also deep respect for the people in the room."

Eventually, I said what was on my chest, something they might have suspected but hadn't heard from me directly, "You were the compromise." Wendy laughed out loud, but I hadn't meant it to be funny.

"I hate to say it that way, but that's what it was," I explained. "There was this sense that we weren't ready, but we can do Darakshan, Silvia, and Wendy. I wanted to bring people with lived experience of poverty onto the board, but the board said no."

I admitted that this all felt icky, and Wendy said she was glad we were having this conversation. "Being brought onto the board felt weird," she recalled.

I asked the question, "How does it feel to be a compromise?" I likened my question to the famous one by W. E. B. Dubois in *Souls of Black Folk*, as he intuited the deeper meaning behind white folks' questions: "How does it feel to be a problem?" (1903, 12).

Silvia said, "I knew walking in the door what I was to you. I understood my currency. I never felt used, by the way. I used the system to get a little bit of change." She continued, "We were the level of comfort for the board at the time. We were the kind of people they were comfortable having as peers. It reminds me of white people and how uncomfortable they are around people of color and how often in the past I have done my best to make them feel comfortable around me—how I dress, how I relate to them, the language I use."

Darakshan hadn't yet reacted or said anything, so I put the question to her directly: "How does it feel to be a compromise, Darakshan?"

"I have lived experience," she started. "I am not there anymore." She went on to say, "The violence is that [we] are being used for proximity to impacted people, but [our] experience is being totally erased. The board was fully upper middle-class and secure in a way that I am not."

At this point in the interview, I began to feel even more complicit in this dance—this compromise—with the board to find people more palatable because the board wasn't ready to bring poor people to its table. I felt responsible for bringing Darakshan, Silvia, and Wendy onto the board to fulfill our objectives, and this conversation was driving home the fact that we had set aside deeper considerations about what they might bring to us. This was classic tokenism, and I knew how it felt to be a token. What I had done was not okay, and I apologized to them.

"Yanique, do not take responsibility for white supremacist structures," Darakshan urged. "I don't know if CHF would have been a safe place for impacted people at that time. People at the sharpest margins *are* on the board now, and they *are* leading. If we had gone too fast, it may have blown up and been unhelpful and harmful for everyone. Us coming in and being a power bloc to vote on things made the difference. I feel good about that."

Wendy added that she was so glad the board had paused and done some work before bringing people with experiences of poverty onto the board. Otherwise, "we would have fucked people up."

I appreciated Darakshan and Wendy for trying to assuage my guilt, but I still wanted to know if they had been harmed by the foundation. They said that *harm* was a strong word and that many more overt harms were out there in the world. Darakshan opined that "nonprofits are built with a white supremacist structure. And even among people of color, class and respectability show up because that is what it takes to make it in white spaces."

But the fact that worse harms can be found elsewhere doesn't mean the foundation didn't cause some harm. I told them about the retreat with people of color in philanthropy that Resourcing Radical Justice, a new funder collective CHF had cofounded at the top of the COVID-19 pandemic, had organized. Participants talked in similar ways about filtering and parsing their ideas in white spaces, their inability to show up as their full selves, and the harm that this caused. I asked again, "Did CHF cause harm?" All three said no.

I decided not to push any further. Whether they agreed with the use of the word *harm* may not be meaningful. Maybe it says more about me and my compulsion to name and root out harm than it does about them. But I do believe it is important to acknowledge that even though CHF is an anomaly in philanthropy, we continued to embody cultural norms born of white supremacy that needed dismantling. Tokenism is one of those norms. I did find it curious that these radical women of color defended the pace of CHF's transformation. It took seven years from the time I wrote my ninety-day report after joining the foundation in 2012, in which I called out the lack of class diversity on the board, to the time the first community members with recent lived experience of poverty joined the board. I think it's absurd that it took that long. I guess we will agree to disagree.

"When did you find your voice?" Silvia asked us all, taking over the facilitator role. I described Roberta's comment about Black people committing crime in her neighborhood as my turning point, and for the first time I told Darakshan the story about how her unprompted observation of Roberta in 2017, right before my final meeting with Roberta, had given me the courage and conviction I needed during that meeting. Darakshan, who had been off video, turned on her camera. She remembered Roberta's comment as being anti-Blackness 101 and admitted that she hadn't interjected in the moment because she wasn't yet sure of the foundation's norms.

Her eyes darted from left to right repeatedly as she described to us her disbelief when she heard the comment. "I am trying to understand the norms here." She looked around as if someone were following her. "Do I call it out? In a community meeting, Roberta would have gotten shut down," she said emphatically. We all laughed and nodded. "The community would have said, 'You have to get out.' She would have been crying," Darakshan joked as she reiterated how confused she had been in the meeting.

Wendy described finding her voice as "an accumulation of multiple moments." After Nia, the foundation's healing justice associate, had brought the Tree of Life tool to a board meeting in 2019, and each board and staff member used it to tell stories about the ways in which race, class, and gender shaped our lives, she thought, Okay, I can now bring my full self in. Wendy also reflected on a breakfast meeting with Nia and Darakshan, when Nia had asked them both to tell their personal stories. Wendy said it made her feel human.

Silvia also pointed to the Tree of Life exercise as pivotal. During the exercise, Kendra had shared that on her first day of work at the foundation in 2014, she was becoming nervous about where her family would live. It dawned on Silvia how little we knew about each other. She said Kendra's story made her feel like a hypocrite. "Here we all were, working together to advance racial justice for Black people experiencing housing instability, and a staff member was such a person and we didn't even know it."

While Darakshan, Wendy, and Silvia are not Black and had started at CHF as a compromise between me and the board, they ended up being allies in and advocates for CHF's transformation, which now centers Black people, racial justice, and communities most impacted by systemic racism and economic injustice. I couldn't have done it without them. They dropped hints—"I thought we were an antiracist organization?"—that gave me permission to speak up. They echoed my own experience in white spaces—"I know how Yanique feels. I, too, have experienced microaggressions." And it was Wendy who said to the board in 2018, "What about a fifty percent plus one community-driven board?" I wasn't at that meeting, but I heard from Wendy afterward that the question had caused a commotion. But at least it got the conversation going.

Guiding Questions:

- What compromises have you made in your life and work?
- Was anyone (including you) harmed in the process? If so, how can you make amends?

---

1. This term was defined in the 1980s by UC-Santa Barbara professor Cedric Robinson who recently passed away. He argued that the development, organization, and expansion of capitalist society pursued essentially racial directions.

14

PULLING BACK THE CURTAIN ON PHILANTHROPY

> What remains unexamined ... are frank conversations about where that wealth came from, why it's held back from public coffers, how it's invested as an endowment, and who gets to manage, allocate, and spend it.
> —Edgar Villanueva, *Decolonizing Wealth*

A FAINT SMILE BRUSHES ACROSS MY LIPS EVERY TIME TONY TELLS THE story of his first encounter with Consumer Health Foundation (CHF). Tony has HIV. The way he frames it, he lives with a compromised immune system. Diagnosed on Friday the 13th in July 1990, the year before Magic Johnson disclosed his own diagnosis, Tony was only thirty-one, and the doctors had given him ten or so years to live. "It was like a death sentence that hovered over my head," he recalls. Up until that point, he had experienced too much trauma for ten lifetimes, much less one. At age six, he mourned the death of the man he called Dad. Later, he witnessed the attempted murder of his mother and suffered physical and sexual abuse. As a child, he also coped with a speech impediment and somehow survived the brutality of poverty in southeast DC. At the time of his HIV diagnosis, he was experimenting with crack cocaine and engaging in sex work to make ends meet.

Tony is the eldest of six children and the only boy. He was close to his mother when she was alive and is still close to his sisters, especially the eldest. The night of his diagnosis, he had gotten high and had a vision of his mother and sisters screaming after finding him dead under a trash can, overdosed on crack. He called out to God, "I'm scared. I'm scared I'm going to die." In that moment, something came over him. He heard the words "I'll teach you how to live." Tony is now sixty-four and both a cancer and HIV survivor. Because of his fight to live, he often says he has no time to waste doing things that don't bear fruit. Tony is now one of fourteen members of CHF's Board of Trustees.

When I met Tony, he was a member of the speaker's bureau at Miriam's Kitchen (MK), a nonprofit with a mission to end homelessness. He learned from MK about CHF's Foundation Learning Days, a popular education series on philanthropy designed for community members with lived experience of housing instability and low-wage work. He wasn't sure he wanted any part of it. He had heard of some local foundations through his part-time work as an usher and shift manager at Ford's Theatre, but he had never had this kind of contact with a foundation.

Why would he? In Anand Giridharadas's book *Winners Take All*, we learn that many of those on the forefront of social justice philanthropy—the "winners"—are often former consultants bred by the likes of Goldman Sachs and McKinsey. Tony wouldn't be considered a winner. He was Black, poor, gay, and sick. The winner in him who mentored others with HIV and helped people who are homeless find housing is not the type of winner that foundation boards seek. They recruit the wealthy, the powerful, the formally educated—those who have limited or no lived experience with the social issues they tackle through board service. Apparently, you can address problems you know very little about.

Tony had come across MK after a leaky ceiling in his bedroom went unchecked, causing itty bitty mushrooms to sprout in the carpet below and mold spores to invade his closet. He had a housing voucher through Catholic Charities and his case manager was trying to help, "but she was young and inexperienced," he says, "and not moving fast enough." The management company patched up the problem but never got to the root. He started having breathing problems, and the five spots the pulmonologist found on his lungs scared him. He didn't mean any harm, but he told his case manager, "You need to get me the fuck out of here."

Catholic Charities handed his case over to MK, and they helped him find a unit with a balcony in a posh building near the Watergate Complex in Foggy Bottom. The spots on his lungs went away. He joined MK's advocacy team, from whom he learned about a series being hosted by CHF to pull back the curtain on philanthropy. He decided to check it out, thinking, "Maybe I can get something out of it to boost my advocacy work." He had a conversation with Kendra, CHF's program associate, who offered to send him a taxi the morning of the meeting. She also let him know there would be a small stipend. He rejoiced privately. "You ain't said nothing but a word. Let's do this! Let's find out what this is!"

Tony walked into the first-floor conference room of the building housing CHF's offices. A few minutes before, he had stepped out of a taxi and realized that he had passed the building several times. He used to live nearby and loved the embassy buildings that spoke of faraway places he might never see. Kendra was the first person to greet him. "She looked like she could have been my niece," he recalls. He remembers her as welcoming and knowledgeable. He pushed the heavy glass door open and entered the recently renovated lobby. "The aesthetics were beautiful," he reminisces. "It looked like it was going to be okay for a Saturday." When he entered the conference room, Qaadir, another participant, introduced him to me. Tony had missed the first session the week before because he had a conflict. Between HIV, cancer, and housing advocacy, there was always one.

I was nervous that day, just as I had been during the first session. I am hyperaware of my privileges, and when I meet someone like Tony, I wonder what he thinks of me. Am I approachable? Is my middle-class socialization causing harm? I was also nervous because I had to give opening remarks for the second session, designed to deepen participants' understanding of philanthropy, but I was doing it in Spanish, a language I love and have studied but do not yet speak fluently. I wanted to connect with the Spanish speakers in the room.

Tony was also nervous. He felt behind because he had missed the first session, and top of mind for him was to answer the question, "What am I really here for?" He took his seat and listened to the facilitators as they opened the meeting with centering affirmations. He heard the Latina sisters speaking in Spanish (simultaneously interpreted into English through his headset) about the importance of language justice. He had dated a guy from Nicaragua, who died from a brain tumor, and his grandmother had married a Mexican man, so he felt immediate kinship with them. He heard words and phrases like *anti-Blackness*, *reparations*, and *dismantling white supremacy*. He thought to himself as he looked around, "Where the hell am I?" He says his jaw dropped when I addressed the audience of about fifty people. "This young, beautiful Black woman is the president and CEO?" It was too much too quick, he recalls, describing what was going on in his mind as "a quiet tsunami of a revolution." The more he listened, the more he felt grounded.

Mainstream philanthropy has a pretty good reputation: Wealthy white people work hard to make their money. Then they form foundations to give a lot of it away. That's the story. But the underbelly of the whole philanthropic enterprise is rarely exposed: The money earned by wealthy white capitalists is often earned on the backs of people of color, and philanthropy provides these capitalists with a tax haven. And those who have little incentive to dismantle structures like racism and capitalism fill the seats on philanthropic boards. Only those in the sector with an analysis that centers racial capitalism can clearly articulate the contradictions that these Learning Days were designed to expose. Why share this perspective with community members who experience homelessness or chronic underemployment? Philanthropy needs upending, and CHF believed that together with community members, we could fuel that disruption.

Tony missed the popular "Wealth Inequality in America" YouTube video that our facilitators, Two Brown Girls, had played in session one. The video reveals just how different Americans' imagined wealth inequality is from real wealth inequality, in which the richest 1 percent of Americans at the time of the video's release in 2012 owned 40 percent of the wealth and made 380 times what the average worker did (Politizane 2012). Throughout the six-minute video, the room buzzed with the sounds of whispers, sighs, and air sucked through teeth. Eyes widened. Heads disapprovingly shook from left to right. Shoulders fell. The robust conversation after the video ended let us know we had struck a chord. It was these wealthy Americans, largely white men, who were benefiting from philanthropy's unspoiled reputation, yet many had made their money at the expense of Black and Brown low-wage workers. Each time Ford, Kellogg, Gates, Rockefeller, and Robert Wood Johnson Foundations gave a grant, they reinforced the tale of white men who worked hard, were richly rewarded for that effort, and gave away their money to help those less fortunate.

In the second session, Tony and his peers negotiated power

and conflict on a make-believe Board of Trustees. They worked together to develop the values to guide their philanthropic strategy, and then began the process of making actual grants using a $20,000 pot of money that we had reserved for this exercise. They learned about other foundations working to transform themselves and discovered opportunities to become involved. At the end of the session, I invited interested members of the cohort to apply for four slots on CHF's board.

One woman who had experienced chronic homelessness interrogated me: "Why did it take so long for CHF to extend this invitation?" She then exclaimed, "You said CHF has been around for twenty-five years!" I admitted that we had been working so hard on racial diversity, equity, and inclusion that we had left economic issues behind. I felt defensive and fought the impulse to remind her that CHF was probably one of very few private foundations in the country taking this step. I wanted to tell her about my early efforts to bring impacted community members onto the board, a proposal that didn't make it out of the Governance Committee. I almost said, "Believe me, I tried!" But I had learned from my days doing community-based research in communities like Flint and Atlanta to take the heat when community members give it. It was deserved.

The third session in the series marked the twenty-ninth anniversary of Tony's diagnosis. It was Saturday, July 13, 2019. It hit him at the end of the session when everyone formed a circle and held hands. He felt compelled to share his truth and felt safe to do so as a Black gay man "standing on the shoulders" of those who had gone before him, like James Baldwin, whom he calls Jimmy. Tony had known the pain of being in the closet. The places that he had gone for solace—church and school—did not provide it. He said, "We die in our misery and shame." However, this group of people embraced him, and he left feeling as though he had found another family. He had found home. He says he will never forget the atmosphere and chemistry that were in the room—the humility in the room.

When I ask him why he uses such strong words—*home* and *family*—to describe an experience with strangers, he says, "I got to be my authentic self, and we were talking about the things I cared about—how we advance Black people who struggle, who live in the hood, who live in substandard housing, people who are unemployed. These issues touch me personally." Along with eighteen others, Tony applied for one of four seats on the CHF board and was one of eleven selected for an in-person interview with members of the Nominations and Governance Committee.

As he matriculated through the process, Tony also reviewed grant proposals at the invitation of the former executive director of the Weissberg Foundation, Hanh Le. He had met her at the Foundation Learning Days, where she had joined me on a panel along with Nat Williams, the executive director of the Hill-Snowdon Foundation. We discussed how we negotiate the contradictions inherent in philanthropy. The key one being that while we deploy the resources we steward to benefit our communities, the amassing of those resources may have caused our communities harm.

Tony is now in his fourth year on the CHF Board of Trustees and has chaired the Strategy Committee. He also served on the Strategic Planning Committee during his first year. In one discussion, he expressed his appreciation for the staff's draft vision statement, which read, "Black people and people of the global majority live powerfully, abundantly and beautifully in healthy, self-determined communities free of social, economic and ideological violence." "But," he said in response, "this vision sounds pie in the sky." After a pause, he asked, "Where is the fight?" He had echoed Frederick Douglass, who said in 1857, "Those who profess to favor freedom and yet deprecate agitation are people who want crops without plowing the ground. They want rain without thunder and lightning. They want the ocean without the roar of its mighty waters. The struggle may be a moral one or it may be a physical one, or it may be both moral and physical, but it must be a struggle."

As a result, we developed a new approach to our work, and CHF's vision statement now includes a statement that reads, "While our vision is utopic, it will not be achieved without a fight. Therefore, we will fight, and we will stand in solidarity with those who are also fighting for their lives." With his question, Tony had singlehandedly upped the urgency and deepened our resolve. He had gotten behind philanthropy's curtain, looked around, and declared that the polite version of philanthropy—in the face of these massive and merciless systems—is no longer welcome in his community.

Folks with HIV who are homeless need Tony. He tirelessly advocates with them and on their behalf. But philanthropy needs him too. When Tony is at the table, we have the possibility of effectuating deep and lasting structural change. We get to build the skills that it will take to work across class differences, and the clarity with which we see the problem and potential solutions is sharper. And while we all benefit when that happens, Tony and the millions of people of color struggling under the weight of poverty have that much more to gain if we get it right—and that much more to lose if we don't.

GUIDING QUESTIONS:

- If more people like Tony join philanthropic boards, in what ways might fear and pushback manifest?
- When people who actively experience poverty are in your spaces, what fears or doubts about them live inside of you?

15

TREE OF LIFE

> Stories have been used to dispossess and to malign. But stories can also be used to empower, and to humanize. Stories can break the dignity of a people. But stories can also repair that broken dignity.
> —Chimamanda Ngozi Adichie, "The Danger of a Single Story," TED

OUR HEALING JUSTICE ASSOCIATE WAS THE ONE WHO INTRODUCED US to Tree of Life, and for a little more than two years, from 2019 until 2021, she facilitated our board and staff in telling life-giving stories. At each board meeting or board and staff retreat, we gathered in dyads to share our stories about how race, class, gender, and societal forces shaped our lives, and then two or three people would volunteer to plot on a timeline a moment in their personal history that exemplified the larger themes in their story.

Each time we did this exercise in dyads, I told the story about growing up in Jamaica and how my grandparents on my mother's side worked with their hands—as a seamstress and a carpenter. I talked about how my parents migrated to the United States for opportunity in the 1980s during a period of instability in Jamaica and the low-wage work they found themselves doing to make ends meet. I talked about how my mother said she felt out of her body for the first several months in the United States. She would drive around town to go to work or the grocery store in a sort of daze, thinking to herself, What am I doing here?

I talked about how my parents believed their sacrifice would lead to new possibilities for each of their children. I became the president of a foundation. My middle sister is an accountant who has used her culinary training to launch a food and event-planning business. The baby, who is now the mother of three girls, is an epidemiologist turned health researcher on food supply chains in Kenya, Uganda, and Rwanda, and is now a midwife in training.

When it was my turn to place my story on the timeline, I walked around the conference room table to the long sheet of butcher paper mounted on the wall with masking tape. Our healing justice associate had drawn a timeline from left to right using a black marker. I placed my sticky note with the year "1985" scribbled on it near the center of the sheet, the year that our family migrated, and then turned around to face the group. I talked about how I had the typical markers of success—income, education, and homeownership—but questioned, "At what cost?" By all accounts, America had been good to me, but I questioned if it had been worth the cost of coming here and becoming Black. My friends who had never left Jamaica had created fulfilling lives on the island as doctors, teachers, and lawyers minus the self-hatred that living in an overtly anti-Black country imparts, the incessant in-your-face reminder of your place in the caste system. Was it worth it, this price that my parents and I had paid?

Each of us told stories like this about larger societal forces—in particular, race, class, and gender—and how they intersected to create the person we had each become. The roots of this Tree of

Life were the stories about our grandparents—what they did for work, whether paid or unpaid; where they lived and whether they owned or rented; and how Grandma's work might have been different from the work of men in the household. The trunk of this Tree of Life was the story of our parents—how the work of the mother or female guardian was viewed in the family, whether they were immigrants, and what they did for a living. The fruit of this Tree of Life was our own story—how our family's economic situation affected us, the kind of work we have done, and where we have lived. There were also questions about racial and ethnic patterns in our family histories; how major economic and social upheavals, such as the Great Migration and the Great Depression, had impacted our families; and the barriers our families faced in terms of racism, sexism, anti-Semitism, ableism, classism, language, and literacy.

In my first Tree of Life dyad, I sat across from Tanya, a Black board member, as she told stories about her coal-mining family in West Virginia. What was that discomfort I felt as she spoke? It was dissonance. I had merged the coal mining industry and all its abuses with the lives of white poor people. I had internalized a narrative strategy that erased Black people from rural America and its "hard-working Americans."

Board members David H. and Dave Z. shared a lighthearted exchange about growing up in New York. David H., a Black man in his sixties, spoke about learning at a very young age what it meant to be Black, poor, and a product of public housing. He also shared that his parents used to work for some Jewish people in the garment district, while Dave Z., who was Jewish, let us know that his family owned a clothing store on the lower east side of Manhattan. Though these two families likely never knew each other, the racialized trajectories embedded in their exchange were not lost on me—David H.'s family could have worked for Dave Z.'s family. However, the reverse would probably never be true—that Dave Z's white family worked for David H.'s Black family.

Aydin, a Turkish American Muslim man, told the story of his life after 9/11 and how he got repeatedly stopped in the airport because of his middle name, Omar. Overnight, he went from enjoying whiteness to being a person of color. Art, also a white man, shared how a cop in the eighties safeguarded his white privilege, telling him to get back in his car and leave Rhode Island Avenue, Northeast, which was a Black poor neighborhood at the time. He had just moved to DC, and when he went beyond the boundaries of his race and class, he was quickly redirected.

Kendra told her story of impending displacement from public housing. On her first day of work at the foundation, February 10, 2014, she had begun to panic about where she would live. Not one of us knew this experience until she told her story in 2019. Like Kendra's story of displacement, others shared stories of having to move against their will. Hanh's family fled Vietnam after Saigon fell. Her father was a pilot, so they flew to nearby Thailand and sought asylum in the United States. Alan's mother's family fled Austria in 1939 before the borders completely closed during World War II.

Dilcia escaped from Central America under threat because of her activism, and Silvia migrated to the United States as an undocumented immigrant, crossing the border with a coyote smuggler to reunite with her mom, who had crossed four years before. Others also told migration stories: Darakshan, whose family came from Pakistan, and Nivo, who came alone from Madagascar. Still others told stories of disorientation, not because of displacement, but as a result of moving from the safety of Black school spaces to white spaces. Tonya and Temi both talked about leaving affirming all-Black school environments to attend white or mixed-race schools that lacked warmth and care.

We told stories of fight: Ria's activism in the Philippines, Tony's efforts to make life better for those surviving on the margins, Robert's struggle for universal housing rights, and Lisa's use of media to push back against racist propaganda in high school, a fight she had in her because of women in her family like her grandmother, who had made the decision to walk off the land where her mother was a sharecropper and make her own way. We told stories of hope and resilience: Wendy's family business dating back to 1895 and what it afforded her in terms of a solid education, Nia's story of the Affordable Care Act and how it enabled her family to get health insurance coverage, and Yazzmine's epiphany that she could have more out of life than the typical success markers.

These were the stories we told. Not that we hadn't told them before, to ourselves or others, but we hadn't told them to each other. How can we do the transformative work of race, class, and gender justice without unpacking these stories together? What better way to grapple with these systems of oppression than to bear witness to how these systems show up in the most sacred of places—in our own lives and the lives of our families. There really is no other way to transform. We might think we can skip this part because "there is work to do." This, too, *is* the work.

An article in *Stanford Social Innovation Review* points to the use of "professionalism" as coded language for white supremacy in the workplace. While the term *white supremacy culture* is currently being debated amongst movement builders (Villarosa et al. 2023), the SSIR article's author Aysa Gray suggests that "professionalism centers productivity over people, values time commitments, accomplishes tasks in a linear fashion, and often favors individuals who are white and Western. In contrast, polychronic cultures, while still able to get tasks completed, prioritize socialization and familial connections over economic labor. Within black and immigrant communities, there is often a deep ancestral connection to polychronic cultural orientation" (Gray 2019). Workplaces steeped in white supremacy often value speed (except when it comes to taking radical action for justice), transaction, and efficiency at the expense of deep relationship building and trust. Even in philanthropy, a word that literally means "love of people," these norms prevail.

A different approach to philanthropy that values relationship will require us to slow down and reconsider the consequences if someone or someplace or some being will get hurt. A different approach to philanthropy means that relationships matter just as much as our programs and outcomes, or even more—relationships not just to other people but also to the planet. And when the impulse to recoil from radical change shows up in ourselves (and it will), relationship and trust allow us to go further together than we otherwise would. People ask me, "How did you do it? What mechanism did you use to move your board?" I rarely have the answer they are looking for. There is no checklist or prescription. But I can say this: Deep and sustained *relationship building* in our movements for social justice is directly related to the change we seek to make in the world. We can't fight massive systems on the outside if we are weakly connected on the inside.

GUIDING QUESTIONS:

- How comfortable are you telling personal stories in professional settings? What is the risk if you do?
- Do you agree with the author that relationship building is core to the change we seek? Why or why not?

16

FREQUENTLY ASKED QUESTIONS

> We often avoid the question of whether something is worth
> doing by going straight to the question "How do we do it?"
> In fact, when we believe that something is definitely not
> worth doing, we are particularly eager to start asking How?
> —Peter Block, *The Answer to How Is Yes*

BY THE SUMMER OF 2019, CONSUMER HEALTH FOUNDATION (CHF) board and staff members were deep in our work to decolonize CHF. We were telling stories about how systems of oppression showed up in our lives and our family's lives. We were building relationships with community members with lived experience of poverty through the Foundation Learning Days. We were exploring participatory grantmaking and making plans to give community members control of our major grant portfolio, and we were interviewing community members for four of fourteen slots on the CHF Board of Trustees. Wendy had proposed 50 percent + 1 community leadership and had gotten pushback, so the board settled on making just four slots available. It was now time for me to propose compensation for these new board members. CHF had never compensated board members, but it was my belief that the community-based board members should receive a stipend to facilitate participation and not just $50, $100, or even $250 per board meeting. I proposed $10,000 per year.

I began making the rounds to test the idea. I shared the idea with Silvia, the chair of our Governance Committee, while she was recovering from an accident at home. I sat at her small, round dining table to talk it through. She said in her community work, stipends had changed community members' willingness to fully invest in a project that she had been a part of. The community members in her project wouldn't do more than the minimum without compensation. Silvia was one of the people most committed to the idea of bringing on community members, so I assumed she would be open to a healthy compensation, but she was not. I rebutted, "I have worked in communities where stipends were provided, and I did not have that experience." Our exchange had some heat in it. I remember the frustration as I walked down Fourteenth Street back to my car and thinking, You cannot use one experience with one community to make a blanket statement about communities' motivations.

I hosted a Zoom conversation with Darakshan, Wendy, and Silvia in 2021 to hear about their experiences on the Board of Trustees as organizers and advocates. Silvia acknowledged then that she had struggled with the stipend proposal for the new community-based board members and referenced our heated exchange. She revealed that she had talked to Darakshan after she and I had spoken and asked, "How come I don't get this?" She was not the only one to ask this question. She also admitted to thinking that the dollar amount was much too high, another common response from board members. She said that even though she knew that people can make millions per year sitting on corporate boards, she had never been paid for community work and believed that community work should be free. She confessed, "I had to come to terms with the fact that I serve because financially I can."

Others also had a hard time with the stipend amount. Alan, a white man, asked, "Are we overprivileging community members?" He said something to the effect that community members might feel as if they had hit the jackpot by making it onto CHF's board. I replied that I did not believe $10,000 per year would overprivilege any of the community members we were interviewing. Some were dealing with housing insecurity at the time of their interview. Even with this stipend, they would still be living in poverty. Though Alan was most concerned about the monetary privilege that community members on the board would have compared to their counterparts not serving on the board, I had come to accept my sphere of influence. I couldn't and wouldn't stop the efforts underway to change our institution just because I couldn't change every circumstance.

Dave, also a white man, asked a perplexing question: "If I lost my job, would I be eligible?" As a white man with a college degree and extensive social networks, and a rising star in his field, job loss would mean something entirely different than chronic unemployment and racialized poverty. He also asked if compensation would phase out over time if a community member's economic position improved. As much as I wanted to be hopeful, I knew the American rags-to-riches story was rare.

Research tells us that we essentially remain in the same social categories that we are born into. As a matter of fact, an explosive study published in the *New York Times* in 2019 found that Black boys raised in America, even in the wealthiest families and living in some of the most well-to-do neighborhoods, still earn less in adulthood than white boys with similar backgrounds (Badger et al. 2018). Nothing I knew about social mobility for Black people suggested that it was worth considering the possibility that a community member would become so much better off than when they started.

These are just the questions and concerns that I can remember. Except for a couple of people, not many board members were excited that we might get a chance to practice equity, which sometimes means that another person or group will get a benefit they need, to correct the impact of systemic racism and economic injustice, while those who are less impacted won't get it. There were also Black middle-class people who admitted that they, too, could use $10,000, but they understood the rationale and would support the direction. As Black people, they had financial struggles that $10,000 could help alleviate. Members of the Black middle class often trail our white counterparts in terms of home values, assets, and income and are embedded in communities that collectively never have enough. But even though they understood, they were not vocal supporters. Their support felt lukewarm.

As I write these pages, I am experiencing all over again the fatigue of the summer of 2019, yet this fatigue was not caused by external-facing engagement and not primarily caused by white people. This pressure was coming from inside, and most everyone was a person of color. There were questions about tying compensation to benchmarks, such as meeting attendance, or providing it only if someone needed it, such as if they had to miss work to attend a board meeting. I pushed back. These suggestions felt like rules within federal programs that punish people living in poverty by imposing work requirements and shaming them into proving need. I was committed to the idea that we would provide $2,500 every quarter without question to support participation and compensate community members for their expertise.

Considering that nothing was being taken away from existing board members (they had never been compensated), I was exasperated by the barrage of questions, which ranged from "How do we define a community member? Am I not a community member?" to "What are the risks associated with compensation?" The board does have a fiduciary responsibility to ask tough questions about financial decisions. This is one of its key roles. But the number, intensity, and narrative underpinning of the questions sounded to me like the same narratives about poor people of color that drive harmful public policies. It was then that the gravity of the shift from external accountability to internal decolonization made sense. We had our own work to do. Even though we were considered progressive in philanthropic circles, we had ingested racism and classism and spewed it back out when under duress.

To give you a sense of the questions that were asked and my responses, I am sharing excerpts from a memo that I wrote to the board in FAQ style for consideration leading up to the vote on the four people who were being recommended for board membership and the compensation policy that I had proposed. Here are the questions and my responses verbatim.

HOW ARE WE DEFINING COMMUNITY MEMBER? For the purpose of the 2019 recruitment cycle, we are defining community member as a person of color in the DC metropolitan area who has recent lived experience (<5 years) with housing instability (e.g., homelessness, housing voucher or rental assistance, multiple moves because of rent prices), low wage work as an adult (e.g., making minimum wage, working for tips, experience with wage theft), and unemployment or underemployment for long periods of time (e.g., looking for work for 6 months or more). We also asked about personal lived experience with receiving public benefits (e.g., SNAP, TANF). This definition allowed us to recruit community members who live at the sharpest intersection of race and class—the very people whose lives we hope would be better off because of the work of the Foundation.

. . .

WHAT IS THE AMOUNT UNDER CONSIDERATION? $2,500 per quarter for each of the four community-based board members. This equals $10,000 per person per year or $40,000 per year in aggregate.

WHAT IS THE PURPOSE OF THE COMPENSATION? Because of community members' social location, there are supports they may need in order to show up fully and be present for the strategic work of the Board of Trustees. This includes direct financial compensation. These supports are similar to the ones all people need in order to engage in work. All of us, because of our own social locations, already have access to many of these supports. There is expertise that community members have that we do not have, and compensation is a tool that we have to facilitate participation.

Each quarter, board members are expected to participate in a board meeting and at least one committee meeting. Board members are also expected to prepare for meetings, provide advice to the CEO upon request and participate in other ways (e.g., speak at a conference or meeting, meet with a constituent, etc.) that support the mission of the foundation. Board members also participate annually in a full-day board and staff retreat, learning journey and/or an annual meeting.

DO WE ALL GET THE COMPENSATION? WOULD A CURRENT BOARD MEMBER GET IT IF THEY FALL ON HARD TIMES? The members of the current Board of Trustees have a level of privilege that is very different from that of the new community-based board members. CHF's diversity matrix indicates that 11 of the 13 existing board members (including the CEO) who participated in our 2019 survey have never had any of the experiences listed above. Equality would suggest that all board members qualify for the compensation. Equity suggests that those who have been most marginalized by racism and economic injustice receive it.

One board member suggested that there might be current board members for whom a stipend would facilitate participation. That may be the case, and I would encourage the Board to consider the full range of what constitutes a board member's socio-economic position, including education, income, access to social networks that facilitate social mobility, access to credit and the accumulation of assets, including retirement accounts.

WHAT DO THE BY-LAWS STATE? The by-laws state: The Trustees shall serve without compensation or other remuneration, <u>except</u> the Board may from time to time authorize that one or more of its members may be reimbursed for expenses incurred in serving as a Trustee or be compensated for services rendered to the corporation, subject to the provisions of Section 7.2. Section 7.2 provides guidance for compensation above $100,000.

IS THIS FINANCIALLY FEASIBLE? The finance and investment committee members discussed this question and there are different views. One committee member suggested that we might spend down faster. Another committee member suggested that if we don't have $40,000 to do this, then we are not viable.

Our director of finance recalculated CHF's spend down projections to help answer this question. Assuming a 5% average return over the next 10 years and assuming that CHF's budget increases by 3% each year due to inflation, the year that the foundation might spend down (i.e., 2031) does not change. In other words, given the assumptions, the Foundation will spend down [without additional infusion of dollars] in 2031 whether we provide this compensation or not.

WHAT BENCHMARKING DATA EXISTS ON BOARD MEMBER COMPENSATION? The Council on Foundations is a source for benchmarking data. The latest information that they gathered on board member compensation is from their 2017 report (data collected in 2016):

- 52% of independent private foundations report compensation to board members
- Within our asset class, 19% provide compensation to board members
- Of those, about half provide to all board members and half provide to some
- For private independent foundations, the median aggregate board compensation and per member compensation numbers (annually) were $96,000 and $15,100 respectively
- Within our asset class, the median aggregate board compensation and per member compensation numbers (annually) were $40,000 and $10,000 respectively

WHAT IS THE PROCESS FOR MAKING PAYMENTS? Our former director of finance made the following recommendations:

- All payments will be reported through the 10-99 process; a W-9 will need to be completed

- Payments will be made via check, ACH or wire on a quarterly basis
- These payments will be reported on the 990 under the section that names board members
- A signed contract should be in place

I am also suggesting that we not make payment contingent upon attendance. The regular rules should follow for attendance. If a board member misses three board or committee meetings in a row, they are asked about their commitment to the Board. If they are unable to make the commitment, then they are invited to resign. This is a process that CHF has used in the past for accountability related to attendance, and it has worked well.

WHAT ARE THE RISKS? DO THE RISKS OUTWEIGH THE BENEFITS? There have been some concerns expressed about the distinction and potentially negative dynamic that could develop because some board members will be financially compensated and some will not. I believe we can mitigate this potential dynamic by engaging in relational work on the front end. I also believe that the questions raised in this process warrant future discussion about equity in practice. Wading into this discussion could be a risk. But, I believe this is the work that we are called to, and the potential benefit of learning and sharing with the field far outweighs the risks.

WOULD COMPENSATION BE SUSTAINED OVER THE BOARD MEMBERS' TERMS? ARE WE CONCERNED THAT WE ARE LIMITING THIS OPPORTUNITY TO JUST FOUR BOARD MEMBERS? The compensation is intended to support the community-based board members for up to three three-year terms. This is the maximum number of terms per the by-laws. This is not the only opportunity for other community members to participate in the work of the Foundation. The staff has planned opportunities related to grantmaking, capacity building, and strategic communications. The staff envisions community-centering occurring throughout the Foundation's work. However, it is true that the other opportunities that we have planned will not include this level of compensation because the level of effort will be significantly lower. One trustee has suggested shorter board terms to allow more community members to participate on the Board of Trustees.

WOULD TRANSPORTATION AND CHILDCARE BE IN ADDITION TO DIRECT FINANCIAL COMPENSATION? IS COMPENSATION AUTOMATIC, OR DO THEY OPT IN IF IT IS NEEDED (E.G., IF SOMEONE HAS TO MISS WORK TO ATTEND)? The compensation is in addition to the other supports (i.e., childcare, transportation, and interpretation) and is designed to be paid automatically each quarter to avoid the potentially harmful situation in which someone has to prove that they need it, a reality that people with low incomes often experience in the institutions they encounter. I have estimated that the childcare, transportation and interpretation costs in 2020 will be $13,000. The majority of this cost is related to interpretation services for a new board member who communicates primarily in Spanish. Childcare would be provided on-site at board and committee meetings and would therefore be available to all board members who need it.

WHAT ARE THE IMPLICATIONS OF THE COMPENSATION FOR THE COMMUNITY MEMBER? This compensation could be transformative because it is rare that community members have the opportunity to access this level of income to support their leadership. However, we realize that community members' public benefits could be compromised by this compensation. The staff has spoken with a benefits attorney who will advise new board members as they balance the compensation with their income requirements for any public benefits they may be receiving. The attorney will be able to talk individually with community members joining the board about what is best for their individual situations.

There may be other implications that we cannot anticipate. The request is for a ceiling of $2,500 per quarter per board member. The board chair and the CEO can then be in conversation with the community-based board member about the implications, including the possibility that another community member may find out about the compensation, which is publicly recorded on the 990. Community members can then decide what is in their best interest as it relates to financial compensation.

GUIDING QUESTIONS:

- The philanthropic sector is often accused of overanalyzing when faced with the opportunity to take radical action. Why do you think this is the case? Whom or what are those in the sector afraid of?
- In what ways do you use prevailing narratives about poor people?

17

WHAT HAPPENED TO FAITH?

The purpose of getting power is to be able to give it away.
—Aneurin Bevan, *Aneurin Bevan*

"Turning over grantmaking decisions to poor people is like giving your child free rein of your bank account. They both make no sense." This was the reaction of a Consumer Health Foundation (CHF) board member's spouse to the foundation's march toward participatory philanthropy—where those most marginalized make decisions about how money is distributed in their communities. It is a most unkind thing to say, but it's probably what most people believe. If children are considered immature in their development, impulsive, and short-sighted, then the analogy is apropos for how most Americans probably view those who are impacted by the violence of poverty.

Instead of heroes who miraculously survive the merciless daggers coming from all sides—humiliating requirements to get access to small sums of money and food, policing of their bodies and movements, and inhumane narratives that you can find in the comments section of any *Washington Post* or *New York Times* article on poverty—poor people of color are not trusted to take care of their own needs, even though they do it day in and day out with their backs against the wall. I can't help but wonder if Faith felt the same way when she quit the CHF Board of Trustees after serving for only six months during the height of CHF's community-centered transformation.

Faith[1] joined the foundation's board after our ten-month search to find board members with legal, human resource, or investment expertise. We especially encouraged applications from people over sixty-five after reviewing our board matrix and noticing that we had a gap in that age group. As a practice, CHF does not recruit new members simply by tapping into existing members' networks as most boards do. We want to cast a wide net to make broader and deeper community participation possible, so we issue a public call for board members. I did meet Faith through a former board member. However, she interviewed for an open slot that year just like many others had.

Faith is a soft-spoken Black woman who was in her sixties and had recently retired. When she interviewed with the Governance Committee, she described her interest in racial justice, her lived experience growing up poor, and her mother's activism even as someone with little means. Given that we were transforming to center community members with recent lived experience of poverty—as evidenced by homelessness; using a voucher to afford housing, unemployment, or underemployment for six months or more; and low-wage work—Faith was the perfect candidate. She had straddled both worlds.

Three months after she joined the board, Faith attended her first committee meeting. She had decided to serve on the Program Committee, which was responsible for deepening the board's understanding of the foundation's efforts in the community and approving (or at times, though rarely, disapproving) the staff's grant recommendations. That night, our senior program officer, Ria, and our program associate, Kendra, made the case to the committee to shift the foundation's grantmaking process and engage in participatory grantmaking, in which members of affected communities—instead of program officers hired by the foundation—would make decisions about how grantmaking dollars are spent. The staff had been relying on the report *Deciding Together: Shifting Power and Resources through Participatory Grantmaking* (Gibson and Bokoff 2018) to guide our case-making. The report defined participatory grantmaking as ceding decision-making power about funding decisions—including the strategy and criteria behind those decisions—to the very communities that a foundation aims to serve.

In response, Faith piped up first, panic in her voice. "What is my role as a board member if we do this?" she implored, referring to the path we were on to cede power. "What is my fiduciary responsibility?" She argued that none of the examples in the report of foundations practicing participatory grantmaking were private foundations with a corpus like ours. They were all organizations that raised their own money to then give it away.

She was right. One of the things that disturbed the staff was the lack of private foundation examples engaging in participatory philanthropy that we could share with the board. This distinction she made is important because there is a sort of hierarchy in philanthropy. Foundations with a corpus have a higher status than those that raise money to give it away. Similarly, those with large endowments get more chances to speak and share their work than those with smaller endowments. I can't tell you how many times I have been asked at philanthropy conferences, "What is the size of your endowment?" It's like being asked at a fancy dinner party, "So, what do you do for a living?"

Others on the committee asked their own questions, mainly about the staff infrastructure to support the approach, which would require recruitment, training, and management of a grant-making committee made up of community members. There were also questions about why we needed additional community participation in our grantmaking given that we were bringing four community members onto the board itself. These were all valid inquiries. I had my own questions. I would have been happy if community members controlled a third of our grantmaking portfolio, but the program staff was advocating for 100 percent community control. We tabled the conversation for the full board meeting, where we planned to have two organizations, AIDS United and Red Umbrella Fund, share their own experience with participatory grantmaking.

As soon as the Program Committee meeting adjourned, people greeted each other and socialized. It is one of my favorite parts of board and committee meetings. The energy is high. The esprit is palpable among the mix of people assembled from all walks of life who joined the foundation at different times and for different reasons. You might see a Black woman with a nonprofit background who has been on the board for eight years chatting with a white man with an investment background who has been on the board for five. People do really enjoy each other. I was talking to a board member when I glimpsed Faith as she briskly walked out the door. She was the first one to leave the meeting. I made a mental note to reach out to her soon. I sensed a question beneath her question about participatory grantmaking: "What is my role as a board member if we do this?" Something in her voice had sounded alarmed.

At the board meeting following the Program Committee meeting, the executive director of Red Umbrella Fund, which supports organizations working on behalf of sex workers, started with a mantra that came out of the disability rights movement: "Nothing about us without us." Sex workers—those most impacted—make up most of the fund's board and committees. She shared her perspective on the process, including that it will not be perfect, you can't take back power after you start down this road, and transparency is important in terms of what powers impacted community members do and do not have. AIDS United also presented its process of involving people with HIV/AIDS as decisionmakers on grantmaking committees. Lessons included paying community grantmakers for their time, bringing as many new people as possible into the process to share power broadly, and using a trusted third-party facilitator to mediate the power differential between staff and impacted community members.

Board members asked questions about the potential for the process to re-create gatekeeping and unhealthy power dynamics between the community grantmakers and the nonprofits receiving funds. In the context of this question, I am always curious about this paradox: these board members are themselves gatekeepers with relationships throughout the nonprofit community. Board members also returned to the question about the labor intensity that would be involved in managing a community-driven process. The Program Committee planned to continue the discussion at its next meeting, and we transitioned from this topic with no utterances from Faith. When the meeting adjourned, she again left abruptly. I made another mental note to reach out to check on her in a couple of weeks. However, I never got the opportunity. Three days later, Faith called.

"I am calling to let you know that I am resigning from the board," she said with pain in her voice.

"Oh no, Faith. Why?" I asked.

"I know myself. I just can't."

"I was planning to reach out to you but wanted to give it a little time. Can we sit down and talk?"

"No, I have made my decision," she said. Again, she sounded distressed.

"Does this have to do with the participatory grantmaking? We still have more thinking to do about it, and we need everyone's perspective to figure out what will work for us."

"I can't. But I do want to say that a board has certain responsibilities."

"And that's why we need to hear your voice. Are you sure we can't go to lunch to discuss this?"

"No, I can't. I will send a formal resignation letter shortly."

"Okay, Faith."

"Bye, Yanique."

I waited for the letter to show up in my email inbox, but instead it appeared one day on top of a pile of mail that had been delivered to my desk. I opened it, hoping for more clarity. "It is with great regret, that for personal reasons, I resign from the CHF board," she wrote. "I want to stress that I very much admire the dedication of CHF staff and board members to issues of racial equity." She continued to say that our decision in 2015 to reject perpetuity and our plans to embrace shared governance with community members was visionary. But she was unable to contribute to the work of the foundation in a way that was commensurate with the foundation's needs and her desire to be of service.

She did not mention fiduciary responsibility as the rationale for her abrupt resignation. I sat at my desk perplexed, her letter in my hand. Maybe that really wasn't the issue after all?

When I announced her resignation at the board and staff retreat the following week, one board member, who also had grown up poor, said, "Good riddance." Faith's questions about fiduciary responsibility followed by her sudden departure suggested that she was uncomfortable sharing power with community members, which may have felt like a rejection of us as a foundation and him as someone who had grown up in public housing. I did not feel the same way. I said to everyone assembled around the table, "As a Black woman, it's hard for me to lose a Black woman in this way. We need everyone for this journey."

I have since accepted that we will lose people along the way. But I continue to wonder, "What happened to Faith?" The easy answer is that she disagreed with giving power to community members and believed that board members should have the final say about decisions related to grantmaking. However, there could be much more to the story. As a person who grew up in poverty, was Faith provoked in some way?

If this were just about board responsibility, as a licensed attorney she could have helped us navigate these waters. As far as I know, there is no IRS rule that gives private foundation boards grantmaking approval authority, but we might have teamed up with our auditors to make sure. We could have gotten to consensus on this over time, or we might have instituted a gap year in which the board maintained final approval authority of community members' decisions just to see what the process produced. So much was possible if this were just about fiduciary responsibility. I can't help but think it was not the only thing at play.

In *Disintegration: The Splintering of Black America*, Eugene Robinson argues that there is not just one Black America. As a result of desegregation, affirmative action, and immigration, "instead of one Black America, now there are four:"

- a Mainstream middle-class majority with a full ownership stake in American society
- a large Abandoned minority with less hope of escaping poverty and dysfunction [sic] than at any time since Reconstruction's crushing end
- a small Transcendent elite with such enormous wealth, power, and influence that even white folks have to genuflect

- two newly Emergent groups—individuals of mixed-race heritage and communities of recent black immigrants—that make us wonder what 'black' is even supposed to mean (2010, 5)

In his book, Robinson scolds the middle-class majority for leaving the large abandoned minority behind. Did Faith want to distance herself from poor people and thus her own past? I had sensed a certain desperation in her voice when she called to resign. "I can't," she said, sounding distressed, when I asked if we could talk. What might have frightened her so?

I recall a book club conversation about *Disintegration* that my husband Ronnie and I hosted with a group of middle-class Black people, both friends and colleagues, in Silver Spring one weekend afternoon. The discussion reinforced Robinson's analysis and proved his point, as this group of Black middle-class people, too, tried to put distance between themselves and poor Black people. I wish I could remember even one such comment to share with you. But I do remember being so frustrated that I painted a scenario in rebuttal: "Let's imagine that somehow all poor Black people got wiped out. They no longer existed in the United States. Something happened and they were all gone. You know that we are next, right? We are next in line to occupy the bottom rung." My admonishment was met with a silence I couldn't read. If this idea—how close we are to the bottom—rings true for middle-class Black people, then maybe proximity to poor Black people was too much of a reminder of Faith's own middle-class fragility. And not just Faith's, but maybe that of all the other Black middle-class people on the board.

I also wonder if Faith felt that community members hadn't paid their dues. Even though she had grown up poor, she rose in the ranks over her career at a prestigious primarily white institution. That probably meant daily code-switching, swallowing insults, and unbearable amounts of microaggressions especially from privileged white interns half her age. This dues-paying member of the Black bourgeoisie may have felt hesitant to share power with community members who had not performed, as she had, for white audiences. Yet this didn't seem like the Faith I had met and built a relationship with over the yearlong recruitment and onboarding process. She said she believed in community agency precisely because she had watched her poor mother fight for poor communities (and win).

I reached out to her colleague who had served on CHF's board and referred Faith to us. She already knew Faith had left the board and said she was really surprised and a little confused about why. It was clear that Faith had the highest regard for me and CHF, she said, and she had tried to get a sense of what motivated Faith's decision. "It didn't seem like one thing," she said. "Maybe just the current board dynamic? It was hard to tell, and I didn't want to press her. I love Faith dearly, and I respect her clear sense of boundaries and priorities, but I can't say I always understand them."

What has been most frustrating for me is that Faith didn't come out and say why she resigned. There is a certain power in that, no? If she felt in any way that her questions about fiduciary responsibility made her appear less progressive, then her "personal reasons" resignation letter allowed her to save face. No one can definitively say why she left. We can only speculate, as I continue to do even now. If Faith had stayed on the board just a few months longer, she would have seen for herself that most of the other board members also had serious doubts about our community-centered transformation. This is typical in philanthropy. The staff wants to go further than the board is willing to go.

Some days, I wonder if Faith just had a literal view of the world. She was a lawyer, and if nothing else, law is about learning the rules and abiding by them—or, if you are wealthy, paying the best lawyers to help you look for the loopholes so you can skirt those rules. I don't know her well enough to know if she was a rule follower or a rule breaker. On other days, I wonder if her sudden departure had something to do with her generation. We specifically sought people who were over sixty-five. Was there something about the time in which she was born and raised that made her feel these new ideas about leadership were untenable? Did she feel she was becoming obsolete when we proposed taking one of her roles away? "What is my role?" she had asked. Was this a question she had been asking in retirement? What is my relevance? Will we all ask this question toward the end of our lives?

I may never know what happened to Faith, but I do believe she represents so much of what existed on the CHF board. The same questions about power and community participation surfaced in many ways across race, class, and gender. Her experience with poverty or possibly feeling on the edge of middle-class status—the precarity of it all—was shared by others who were newly middle-class. What may have happened to Faith may be happening to all of us.

As the CHF board and staff took on racism and capitalism in the world, we were also fighting what these forces have done to us and within us. As we experimented with ways to embed anticapitalist principles in our organization, such as prioritizing relationship building over transactions, we were battling inside ourselves racial capitalism and its insistence that there be a chosen few on top who are primarily wealthy white men who extract from an undeserving class on the bottom that consists mainly of poor Black women. As we explored telling stories about our personal relationship to money, we risked violating one of society's biggest taboos—never talk about your salary and how the threat of losing it scares you to death. As we practiced rituals and ancestral practices in our meetings, some of us might have quietly wondered, Is this professional? I know I felt this question as we engaged in rituals such as singing, adornment, and ancestor naming at a board and staff retreat. Being at CHF was not easy. You didn't get to espouse or dream of a different world while clutching on to the existing order. If you stayed at CHF long enough, your life changed. Or maybe, like Faith, you jumped ship before your contradictions were revealed.

GUIDING QUESTIONS:

- What comforts within the existing order do you cling to?
- What do you need to feel safe as you let go of societal norms that don't serve you or the people you love?

---

1. This name has been changed for several reasons. Most importantly, Faith was only on the board for three months; I didn't know her well.

18

THE VOTE

> It's not about supplication, it's about power. It's not about asking, it's about demanding. It's not about convincing those who are currently in power, it's about changing the very face of power itself.
> —Kimberlé Williams Crenshaw, leading scholar of critical race theory

SEPTEMBER 16, 2019: THE DATE THE BOARD OF TRUSTEES VOTED TO elect community members, two with recent experience of homelessness, onto the board. This day remains etched in my memory. When I sit still and transport myself mentally, I can feel the sensations from that day in my present body. Anxious vibrating energy. The lump in my throat that would not go away. My heart beating.

I worked from home until about 4 p.m. that day, two hours before the third quarter board meeting was scheduled to begin. I stopped by Silvia's house on my way to the office in a Lyft. Silvia was still using a walker following her accident earlier in the year, and I had volunteered to get her to and from meetings. She could have joined by Zoom, but it would not have been the same. Plus, this vote was happening under her watch as the chair of the Nominations and Governance Committee.

Though the board's vice chair, Wendy, and I had hatched and executed a plan to organize board members behind the scenes before the vote, I had no idea how things would ultimately pan out. The board would no doubt accept the Nominations and Governance Committee's recommendation to elect the four new community-based board members, but the tensions regarding the proposed compensation felt unresolved. Alan had suggested a smaller number, maybe $5,000 or $7,000 per year. But I had insisted on $10,000. It needed to be comparable to what we pay consultants but whether it was $7,000 or $10,000 was not as important as the fact that the proposed amount caused so much consternation. For me, it symbolized what was at stake. Were we truly committed to our community-centered transformation and our beliefs about equity?

Silvia and I arrived at the True Reformer Building and walked slowly from the corner of Twelfth and U Streets to the front door—only ten yards, but it felt like a mile. If the board rejected the compensation proposal, what would happen to the last bit of hope I had that society might bend toward people of color living at the sharpest intersection of systems of oppression? It would go to the same place my other hopes had gone to die. I had worked hard over the summer to make the case to the board. I had responded to all their questions. I had proven that we could afford it. And I had what I didn't have before—a strong ally in Wendy. Unlike my proposal in 2013 to elect community members to the board, which had died in committee, this proposal—to elect and compensate—had finally made the journey to the full board.

I deposited Silvia in the oversize conference room and told her that I would be right back. I needed some alone time and took the elevator upstairs. The True Reformer Building housed our cubicles and single office on the fourth floor. The space cost us nothing. The Public Welfare Foundation had purchased the historic building in 1999 and stated in its charter that it would make the building, and its event and office spaces, available at no cost to partner organizations.

The Consumer Health Foundation (CHF) had paused the process of finalizing a lease on an office space after a dozen years in our office suite. It didn't make sense to any of us on the board or staff to spend $2.5 million on a new ten-year lease when that money could be used for programmatic work. At a happy hour gathering of women of color in philanthropy, Candice, the new Black CEO of Public Welfare Foundation, responded enthusiastically to my query about low-cost office space: "We have space!"

The historic True Reformer Building was the first building in the United States designed, financed, built, and owned by African Americans after Reconstruction. The building had been commissioned in 1902 by the Grand United Order of True Reformers, a social change organization, and designed by architect John Anderson Lankford. It was the ultimate testament to the fact that even though Black people had endured some of the worst atrocities during slavery, they reimagined and rebuilt their communities. They did not need others' charity or ideas. They had their our own. Ibram X. Kendi underscores this point in his book *Stamped from the Beginning: The Definitive History of Racist Ideas in America*. He points to what Black people in Savannah, Georgia were saying in the period leading up to abolition: "All Black people needed was to be left alone, secure on their own lands and guaranteed their own rights" (2016, 231). I imagine that the spirit of the true reformers was in the building that night. I wish I had called on them for support. Instead, I was gripped by anxiety as I sat in my cubicle, prepping for the meeting.

A week earlier, Wendy had suggested that we do a bit of organizing before the vote in addition to the organizing I had done all summer. My response was unenthusiastic. "I don't know, Wendy. I need some time to think about it." I had depleted all my case-making energy and wrestled with the feeling that calling around to strong-arm people to vote a certain way seemed disingenuous. I wasn't interested in winning as much as I wanted people to want it too. Maybe that was naive. During the civil rights movement, getting the win was an important precursor to the changing of hearts and minds.

In 1960, six-year-old Ruby Bridges was the first African American to integrate schools in America. She walked by crowds that screamed at her and hurled grown-up insults at a little Black girl. They did not want her—specifically or metaphorically—in their schools. Some would argue that integration went a long way (though not all the way) toward bringing Black people and white people into proximity with each other and created the opportunity for the shredding of the stereotypes that white people had about Black people. Some would argue that too many hearts and minds never changed. But the win was still important: Ruby ultimately graduated from a desegregated school[1]. I enlisted Darakshan and David H. to join Wendy and me in our organizing campaign to see to it that four community members not only became board members but also got compensation worth fighting for. The four of us went to work.

I called most of the Black women. David H. called the white men. Darakshan called Silvia, and Wendy called Deborah. The calls I made to the Black women were awkward and mirrored some of the silence in meetings leading up to the vote. They wouldn't divulge much, though they said they were fine with it. Tanya was surprisingly vulnerable. She admitted her reluctance to approve the compensation amount. She had wondered why this benefit was not being made available to everyone. After some reflection, she recognized the contradiction: "I believe in equity, yet I was advocating for equality." Equity means that one group might get access to more or different resources than others because it needed them. She knew this distinction in theory but lost her way when she was the one who might "lose."

David H. said his conversations had gone well. Two of the white men were enthusiastic and supportive. One still had a lot of questions. Do we have the money to do this? Would this create divisions? Darakshan reported that Silvia agreed to moving forward. Wendy said Deborah also agreed but had concerns about the long board terms we had in place—a total of nine years broken up into three three-year terms. I admit I was wary of this suggestion to shorten terms at a time when community members were joining the board, but Wendy thought the suggestion was genuine and valid, a way to share power more broadly.

By the night of the vote, we had secured ten of the twelve yes votes needed to pass the $10,000 annual compensation for community-based board members, but the anxiety deep in the pit of my stomach would not go away. While a couple of the yes votes were enthusiastic, most felt tentative, and we still had a couple of resisters—white men who were historically confident in making powerful cases on myriad issues. If they made a compelling case against the compensation amount, I was afraid that the folks on the fence might easily shift and the proposed compensation could come down significantly. When I made it back down the elevator to the conference room, I was sure my angst was visible, poking out from under my skin, looking around for company.

I had invited my colleague Nat Williams of the Hill-Snowdon Foundation, who is Black, to speak at the meeting on his foundation's use of power to frame its grantmaking portfolio. He would speak first. We would then review the financial position of the foundation before discussing the new board members and the proposed compensation. In retrospect, inviting Nat to speak about power on the night of the vote was well timed. I wish I could claim that this was my plan all along, to prime the board for the vote by having a speaker join us to talk about community power.

But it was our board chair David H. who had suggested that we involve the board in defining its learning agenda around our community-centered transformation. So we had solicited topics of interest from the board earlier in the year. Most board members selected power from the list of potential topics, which also included healing justice and community organizing. "Power" was not a frequently used word at the foundation, and they wanted to understand its role in our work to advance racial equity.

Nat opened his talk at the front of the grand forty-seater conference room table around which fifteen or so board members and staff were scattered. He said he was surprised that CHF had not used power to frame its work. "I take it for granted that when I talk about racial equity, I am talking about power," he continued, reflecting on CHF's well-known use of the term "racial equity," used by the staff to advocate for undoing policies that created inequities in health, housing, and education by race. "What is my definition of power?" Nat asked rhetorically. "I had to go back to Frantz Fanon and [Paulo Freire's] *Pedagogy of the Oppressed*." He paced the room.

"When I talk about power, I am talking about structural power and how systems interact and use power to produce outcomes. Structural power," he said, "is people organized to win everything they require to achieve their goals. It is people doing a specific thing. Power doesn't just happen. It is very intentional." He also stated that "power is a struggle" and "there are winners and losers." All those who say we can just make the pie bigger would not be happy with this analysis. He continued, "We are taught that power is negative. It is not. What is negative is the goal of the power brokers once they have power."

Nat then asked the room a question: "How many people here feel oppressed?" His question was met with silence. Then Temi braved an affirmative response because of her experience with banks and mortgage companies when trying to buy a home. Nat hesitated, vacillated a bit, and then disagreed: "I would not classify our circumstances as oppression. Having your body in constant threat of violence is oppression. We are not as oppressed as people fighting hunger are." Temi agreed but added that she feels oppressed around police. "Police brutality cuts across class."

I wondered where Nat was going next. He further referenced Fanon and went on to say, "The people do not have access to hegemony. They do not have access to military. However, they do have access to social, cultural, and religious institutions to lead uprisings. You have to deal with power to deal with racial equity. It is not enough to take a policy approach; you have to focus on preparing oppressed people to govern." He then closed with a few rules for how to infuse power into our programs. He read from his PowerPoint slide:

- Trust and support oppressed people.
- People power over policy change. Building people power is most important.
- Struggle and fight are about repairing material conditions and restoring the humanity of the oppressed.
- Be in awe of everything. Embrace the damage and the sacrifice the people on the frontline face everyday.
- Be humble, you can't tell people what they can do.
- Be in solidarity and of service.
- Be courageous, be bold, be persistent.
- Be people focused, celebrate when you see changes in people's lives.

His talk perfectly primed the board for the vote. The true reformers had intervened even though I hadn't summoned them.

An act of grace. I walked Nat out the door and into the hallway as the meeting transitioned and thanked him. Alan left the meeting early because he had a flight to catch and ran into us in the lobby. He, too, thanked Nat profusely. He said that Nat's remarks had had a profound impact on him. After he left, Alan called back in for the vote.

After a review of the financial statements and celebration of a clean audit, our board chair, David H., thanked Silvia for her leadership of the board recruitment process and asked me if I had any comments. My heart, once again, picked up its pace. I had no comments. I had left everything on the field that summer and asked only that board members share their own journeys to this vote.

Silvia started, saying, "As someone who has done organizing, the idea of $10,000 was a lot because you don't see that amount provided to community members. But it is not just about the money; it is a statement that the foundation is making. I think the resources will allow community members to be a part of this."

Then Tanya spoke: "My initial thoughts were, Why doesn't everyone get a stipend? Then I checked myself. That's equality, not equity. If we're going to be true to this work, we have to move forward with this $10,000."

Another board member chimed in: "I want to thank Yanique for how she prepared us. We were very deliberate about this. I was supportive of it but was not sure if it would take away from the foundation's finances. It has to be sustainable."

Then another: "This process took me back to my own personal experience when I was struggling. We extract people's stories. People who are impacted should be able to take material gains from their stories."

And another: "This is about making it possible for people to participate. It is an acknowledgment of what it takes to live in this area."

Then Deborah: "I think we can afford it. If we can't afford $40,000 per year, then we have bigger problems."

Aydin added, "Previous experience with community members on a nonprofit board made me supportive from day one. It would be a shame if they could not participate. I hope this policy will allow it."

Art brought up the rear: "I love that we continue to challenge ourselves. The whole process we are taking is in the unknown. That is uncomfortable for me."

My chest swelled with emotion and pride. Though tough, this process of wrestling with the compensation had forced us to practice equity. It was no longer theoretical but experiential. Having something at stake that hit some people personally (I could use $10,000, too) and struck all the narrative chords about poor people (they don't deserve money without strings) that we all perform to had pushed us into places we had never been. I want this for all progressive foundations—a chance to practice what we preach.

Silvia presented the four new community-based board members and described what they would each bring to the board. Then David H. asked for a motion to accept the recommendation of the Nominations and Governance Committee to invite Tony Burns, Yazzmine Holley-Anderson, Dilcia Molina, and Robert Warren to the Board of Trustees. Tonya moved and Art seconded. "All in favor say aye." The room responded in unison: "Aye." None opposed.

Then Silvia presented the recommendation of the Nominations and Governance Committee to compensate the four community-based board members in the amount of $10,000 each per year. David H. asked for a motion to accept the recommendation of the Nominations and Governance Committee to institute a compensation policy that would provide $10,000 per year for each community-based board member. Jackie moved and Deborah seconded. "All in favor say aye." The room responded in unison: "Aye." None opposed. The room filled with loud applause.

Guiding Questions:

- How do you define racial progress? What does it look like? What does it feel like?
- What racial progress can you celebrate?

---

1. Whether desegregated schools benefited Black people is up for debate. At the time, many considered desegregation a win.

EPILOGUE

Weaponization of White Womanhood continues to be the centerpiece of an arsenal used to maintain the status quo and punish anyone who dares challenge it.
—Ruby Hamad, *White Tears/Brown Scars*

I HAD SUCH GRAND VISIONS FOR THIS EPILOGUE! THE CHANCE TO step back from the writing process and reflect felt like a luxury I wanted to bathe in. I thought about exploring class and gender identity and their intersections with Blackness. I toyed with an idea that I was never able to tease out while writing my dissertation back in 2008. At the time, I was a structural purist and didn't care about individual behavior. Yet in this collection of essays, I outlined examples of individually racist behaviors and finally came to understand what Amy Schulz, a member of my dissertation committee, had encouraged me to consider: that structures inform individual behaviors and individual behaviors in turn maintain structures. "They work together," she had said. I didn't see it then. I see it now.

I also thought about articulating a radical future for philanthropy, providing specific advice to progressive leaders in the sector who don't feel empowered to make the shifts that **if** (formerly Consumer Health Foundation) had made inside our foundation. There were so many possibilities for this epilogue. Unfortunately, I am back to talking about white women. Here is what happened.

I shared excerpts with the white women who appear in this essay collection. Even though I didn't have to do this, I did so for a few important reasons. First, I wanted to make sure I got the events right as I reconstructed these stories. I also took to heart Mary Karr's recommendation in *The Art of Memoir* that memoirists "notify subjects way in advance, detailing parts that might make them wince." She says that in her experience, however, "no one has ever winced" (2015, 120). This was not the case for me. All the white women winced, and that's an understatement. In most cases, they pounced. Even so, I persevered. I felt it was only fair that I give people a heads-up. I appreciate how hard it must be to see one's name in the context of racism, such an emotionally fraught subject.

I also held out hope that maybe, just maybe, these white women with whom I had been in relationship for several years might see this as an opportunity for self-reflection, accountability, and harm repair. I even offered to one woman that we might do something together publicly—speak on the subject, share a podcast episode, write a blog—to raise awareness of the challenges and possibilities of cross-race allyship. She did not take me up on that offer. My body was literally shaking after each email exchange or Zoom call, so aggressive were their responses.

But with support from my partner Ronnie, I began to see the richness of the data they freely provided. It was a perfect, though unintended, social experiment. I had a hypothesis: when confronted with an account of how their racist behavior had impacted me (the independent variable), white women would own their behavior and try to understand it, and in doing so, we might deepen our cross-race relationship (the dependent variable). I admit that my hypothesis was flawed from the outset. Scientists typically build hypotheses based on the existing evidence. *White Fragility* author Robin DiAngelo had already provided countless examples of how white people generally reject any suggestion they might be racist.

However, in my case, there were some moderating variables. In science, this is "a variable that can strengthen, diminish, negate, or otherwise alter the association between independent and dependent variables" (Allen 2017). We were all advocates for social justice and had years of experience working with each other. That counts for something, right? This should counter DiAngelo's existing evidence, thus preserving the relationship between my two variables. So I tested my hypothesis, and I now have "data" to analyze.

Jessica[1] came the closest to proving my hypothesis. Jessica was an employee who had criticized the ninety-day report I had written shortly after joining the foundation. She did not appreciate the tone of my report. She had compared me to the previous white woman leader of the foundation and had said something like, "Margaret would not talk like this. Margaret brings people together." I had bristled because Black women are often tone policed, a tactic used to diminish *what* someone is saying because of *how* they are saying it. When I shared the report with a trusted board member, he didn't understand what all the fuss was about.

I found Jessica easily after all these years. She was still employed at the same foundation she had joined following her departure from CHF. I sent her the email template I ended up using to reach out to everyone. I only sent book excerpts after receiving a response to my initial inquiry.

From: Yanique
Sent: Friday, October 22, 2021
To: Jessica
Subject: Hello from Yanique

Dear Jessica, How are you? I hope you are well. I am reaching out to see if I might meet with you soon. I have completed an essay collection with the tentative title: *White Women Cry and Call Me Angry: A Black Woman's Story to Decolonize Philanthropy*. Before I begin shopping the book to publishers, I am in the practice of talking to people with whom I have had interactions in philanthropy—interactions that are highlighted in the book.

I don't know if you recall an incident that took place in the hallway of our suite at 1400 16th Street, NW when you were at CHF. I mention it briefly in the book. If you are open to it, I would appreciate your review of and feedback on the excerpt, and if you would be willing to talk it through, I would be happy to set up a Zoom meeting or phone call.

As a bit of background: I am sharing stories about my journey in philanthropy, including those interactions with white women that took a toll on me. I was able to take a break after six years (thanks to the board) and used that time to re-establish my center. I was able to return to work with a renewed focus on my own transformation and the transformation of CHF (now **if**, A Foundation for Radical Possibility).

If you are interested, I would love to hear from you.
Yanique

Jessica responded a day or so later, and my heart skipped a beat when I saw her return email in my inbox. This was my first outreach to someone in the book, and her response could be indicative of things to come. She started by saying, "I'm sorry to learn that you have experienced this pattern of interactions with white women in philanthropy and the toll it has taken on you personally and as a leader in the field. And I'm really sorry that one of those interactions was with me. I would be open to reviewing the excerpt from your book that describes the interaction. I'm also open to conversation or deeper listening about the impact it had on you or other types of repair work you recommend."

I had hoped for exactly this kind of openness from my colleagues. I exhaled. It seemed that Mary Karr had been right after all. Maybe no one would wince. I followed up by sending her the excerpt[2]. However, after reviewing it, Jessica replied to say that she didn't recall the specific incident—where it took place and what was said—though she did recall the ninety-day report that was the context for our interaction. Then she asked not to be referenced by name in the book. She didn't mention again any interest in deeper listening about the impact and possible repair.

I still appreciated Jessica's effort at openness. She did not attempt to discredit my recollection and retelling of events, as others did. However, her inability to remember the parts of our previous interaction recalls a point from Derald Wing Sue's book *Race Talk and the Conspiracy of Silence* that I made in the essay "Not That Black." In general, white people are just not as attuned to these incidents because their lives aren't shaped by them. These incidents are tangential. White people can move on with their lives, never recalling what happened, with their sense of their place in the world intact, while for many people of color, these incidents can be central. We move on with our lives, yes, but not without a fair amount of internal flogging ("Why didn't I say something?"), self-doubt ("Did I really hear what I think I heard?"), fear ("I don't want to be labeled as the angry Black person, a label that could threaten my career") or apathy ("Nothing will ever change"). We live a different racial reality.

I also reached out to Karen. This name has been changed because of some of the very personal details that I discuss about Karen's granddaughter in my essay "Not That Black." Her response to my inquiry (before she had even seen the excerpt) was so long that I can't begin to capture all of it here, but I extracted a few lines from what she wrote to help paint a picture.

> I'd also like to make sure that I understand correctly that you consider your essays to be your subjective understanding of the interactions with me, rather than objective truth. As you might expect, I also have a subjective understanding of our interactions, which is as valid to me as yours are to you. And I think it's helpful to have the understanding that the "truth" about the experience would reflect both your perspective and my perspective, and be anchored in facts. ... I understand that you are writing a subjective essay from your own perspective, to which you are completely entitled. At the same time, when it comes to describing our interactions, I am wondering if your essay also reflects objective reality. I've shared the above to give you some examples where your subjective understanding of what happened is very likely different from mine, and where a bedrock of facts must also be taken into account to come closer to what really did happen.

When I reached out to Nicky, she had a similar approach:

> Many of the statements in the excerpts have not been fact checked. Particularly troubling are those statements that

attribute ill-motive to people without any factual basis or are based on rumors and innuendos. I trust that the erroneous and damaging statements listed below will be corrected or removed prior to publication and dissemination.

Both Nicky and Karen repeatedly used words such as *facts* and *objective* in their responses. They were the ones who had the facts—a bedrock of them, according to Karen—and I didn't. In addition, Nicky made statements like "You have no personal knowledge" so freely and confidently, as though there were only one way to know. She did not ask if I had spoken to those involved when I had in fact spoken with dozens of people about the impact of Madye's and Terri's dismissals. In the wake, there was so much loss and grief in our local philanthropic community. So much uncertainty about how we might reconcile and heal. Yet Nicky closed her email by saying, "Ultimately, I know who I am and what I stand for and no one can take that away from me."

In her response, Nicky also pointed to the outcome of the legal case as proof of my wrongness:

> WRAG and all the named defendants denied all the allegations on the record in our court filing, which is in the public record, and you appear to have intentionally omitted any reference to that. The Court never decided whether anyone acted unlawfully when Dr. Henson was terminated. It is irresponsible and harmful to people's reputations to position as true any allegation that has not been proven in a court of law. Furthermore, I was dismissed from the WRAG lawsuit even before the settlement was final.

Instead of curiosity, Nicky used the outcome of a legal system (one that has been shown over and over again to be racist) to bolster her argument. She seemed to suggest that the law was the final arbiter of harm. "You have no personal knowledge," she said.

See, there is this idea upheld by white supremacy that there is such a thing as the objective truth and that it can be achieved only through white people's systems and their interpretation of events. We are experiencing a national version of this right now as school systems, governments, and others work hard to bury the historical record about slavery and racism and the generational impact on Black people. Multiplicity of perspective, especially when it comes to our lived experience as Black people, is not welcomed. Yet in a very interesting way, when that objectivity is in the way of upholding whiteness, somehow these apparent "facts" no longer matter.

Take, for example, drug use and drug dealing. Multiple research studies have found similar levels of drug use and dealing among white Americans and Black Americans. *Washington Post* writer Christopher Ingraham reported on data showing that white Americans are *more* likely to deal drugs. Thus the patrolling of Black neighborhoods to uncover drug-related crimes, without a similar effort in white neighborhoods, is not logical based on the data. Yet white neighborhoods remain largely unpoliced. No one is incessantly looking for drugs there.

It's why Breonna Taylor could be killed while sleeping in her own home but a similar fate may never befall a white woman. Policing a white neighborhood to find the drugs that are certainly there in copious quantities would not align with the white supremacist idea that white neighborhoods are safe and crime-free—that good, moral, superior humans live there. And that Black neighborhoods are dangerous and crime-ridden, the people who live there inherently inferior and immoral. A study of the most common word associations in the media experienced by the average college-educated person in the United States found strong correlations between Black and the word *violent* (Verhaegen, Aikman, and Van Gulick 2011). No word association of such negativity came remotely close for white people.

In my essay "Unhinged," I describe the stress I experienced in my interactions with Roberta, likely one of the top two most painful experiences I had during my time in philanthropy. When I reached out to Roberta with an invitation to review the essay in which she was featured, her response was very straight to the point:

> I appreciate your desire to revisit our conversations as you think about the events and subject you write about. For me, that was a very unhappy time when as a result of your anti-Semitic remarks and refusal to have a simple conversation with me to clarify them I resigned from the Board of a foundation I cared deeply about and had hoped to continue to contribute to. I don't have any desire to revisit that time, read your essay or to be part of or included your book.

After I responded to acknowledge that she did not want to review the essay, she sent another email: "I want to be clear that I do not want to be [in] your book." As I said, this was a common response, which I fully understand. But something about these responses often felt like the bullying I had experienced over the years. There seemed to be a threat, a demand: you will do as I say.

In philanthropy there is a certain niceness that people of color are expected to display even in the face of racism. We are expected to smile and be grateful and keep quiet about what is going on so that philanthropy's "goodwill" can continue, unfettered by the social angst happening out there as corporations and governments bend to the people's demands, even if only for show. In the essay "My Basement," I reveal the promise I had made to myself: I would write to record and expose. It felt like one of the few things within my control. When presented with my story and the opportunity to lean in, each woman chose to back away. Some resurrected their previous attempts at silencing. That's because stories have power. There is an African proverb that says, "Until the lion learns to write, every story will glorify the hunter."

Though I mention Mary only briefly in my essays, her response to the excerpts I shared with her is worth a deeper dive and gives us more insight into the power of story. Leaning on the above proverb, let's imagine that I am the lion. In "Token," I talk about the behind-closed-door conversation I felt I was in with Mary and Chad about Tamara, a Black woman leader. In "A Letter to Freddie Gray," I mention that Mary had called me up to say that using our collective philanthropic voice to write an op-ed on the role of racism in the death of Freddie Gray was not strategic.

When I reached out to Mary to see if she might be interested in seeing the excerpt and discussing it, she responded by saying, "Hi Yanique, it's wonderful to hear from you. I'd be delighted to talk to you and congratulations on your work! I fear my memory may not be the best but I am always happy to talk to you and see what I can help with." Again, I was hopeful that Mary would prove my hypothesis correct—that a white liberal or progressive woman when confronted with what I believed were harmful behaviors could be open to feedback.

I anxiously awaited our Zoom call. I liked Mary as a person and felt no animus as I waited for her image to pop up on the screen. After the initial pleasantries, she asked me to record the session. My heart sank. The request felt adversarial. She opened by saying that she felt sad and that it was never her intent to disrespect or undermine me. She also said she felt confused and disappointed. Regarding the scene I paint in "Token," Mary contended that the meeting I describe with her and Chad was not a meeting to critique Tamara:

> As board members and philanthropy professionals, we were having a lunch to discuss how to build up and support WRAG and make it stronger. ... In that capacity, I think it was appropriate to critique WRAG. ... I spoke to Tamara about that grant and how aspects of it didn't seem to be moving forward. ... Another relevant point for the context you may not know is that [my foundation] gave another significant grant to WRAG ... even under Tamara's leadership, so obviously we thought well of Tamara.

What I believe Mary failed to see was that financial transactions cannot take the place of human connection. For Mary, it was obvious that the money her foundation gave to WRAG was an indicator of her support for Tamara. But Tamara did not feel supported, a point I had made in the excerpt I had shared with Mary. Mary seemed to rely on the financial transaction she had authorized as evidence of her support. Whether Tamara, the human being, felt supported wasn't mentioned. I am offering a "lion story" to counter the "hunter story" that financial gifts from philanthropic coffers are always a gesture of support.

At some point in the conversation, I realized that Mary kept using the term *professional*, which has been surrogate nomenclature for white supremacy in the workplace. I counted. She used the word five times in twelve minutes. "In my professional experience, I think board members do discuss strengths and weaknesses of organizations sometimes outside of the hearing of the director," she said. Other definitions of *professional* that are *not* rooted in white supremacy might mean openly discussing conflict, for example. But again, there is supposedly one objective truth about professionalism, and white leaders in American workplace contexts are the keepers of that truth. We need a "lion story" to counter the "hunter story" about what it means to be a professional.

Mary also said this:

> When you indicated interest in the job I then held, I encouraged you. ... I gave positive feedback to the search committee about you. ... And it was you, who was a new dynamic leader in philanthropy who came to me ... and you said Mary, will you be a mentor. ... I did my best ... to give you ideas and offer suggestions, and I even introduced you to a major leader in philanthropy, Lynn Huntley, who obviously is a Black woman, who was my boss at DOJ and at Ford. She was my mentor. I wouldn't have done that if I didn't have high regard for you.

Another way in which white people often respond to feedback about the racialized impact of their behavior is to talk about what they have done for us, which suggests to me that they are above reproach because of their generosity. What white people fail to understand is that in a relationship, there can be reciprocity, there can be gratitude, and there can, especially in cross-race relationships, be tensions and conflicts that require attention and repair. The fact that Mary had a high regard for me and was willing to introduce me to people and say good things about me doesn't mean that she couldn't also cause harm. In my opinion, her behaviors, which have been groomed out of her social location as a powerful white woman, are likely to cause harm. It is not a matter of if but when. We need a "lion story" to counter the "hunter story" that you can't be racist or cause harm if you are also nice to people of color.

Mary went on to say, "These essays don't reflect the type of professional relationship where I would have thought you would have come to me with your concerns. ... That would have been, to me, a true colleague and a mentor/mentee situation." Moreover, she said, "Had you come to me, we would be much stronger colleagues." Again Mary repeated the word *professional*, because maybe that word would set the rules of engagement. Maybe in her world, two professionals can come to each other and share concerns, discuss, and move on.

In my world, if I share concerns with a professional who is white and more powerful, especially when I can expect to be told during that interaction that my perspective is wrong, then I have put myself and my family at risk if my career gets sidelined. My salary has paid for college tuition and subsidized housing that is too expensive for young adult children and currently supports an aging parent and secondary insurance because Medicare won't pay for everything. That Mary believes she, a white woman, can tell me, a Black woman, what a true colleague means in this context is, in my perspective, the height of racial arrogance. We need a "lion story" to counter the "hunter story" that white women's experience of the world is and should be the standard for women of color.

She then complained that the essay "presents me as a cold white woman with whom you had a distant relationship." In classic form, Mary got to the heart of it. The way I see it, many white women are more concerned about their image and the dissonance between who they believe themselves to be and how we have experienced them. While I hypothesized that liberal or progressive white women could hear how they have caused harm and work earnestly to understand and repair that harm, it would ultimately mean an admission of racism. This is a very difficult proposition. If I believe myself not to be racist, how then can I be racist?

Mary finally said, "In my view the murder of Freddie Gray needed action by us in philanthropy, yet the tradition I generally followed since I had been at Ford and since I had been in the world of philanthropy was that we in philanthropy were actually in a position to undertake a major strategy and direct money to a situation and [my foundation] did that subsequently." Mary's version of "strategy" was centrally about moving money to address a situation, which makes sense given her proximity to power and wealth at very large institutions. My version of strategy, given my social location and my experience at a small foundation, needed reliance on something in addition to money. We need a "lion story" to counter the "hunter story" that speaking out against racism is not strategic.

In *Emergent Strategy: Shaping Change, Changing Worlds*, adrienne maree brown suggests that horrible, racist, sexist, ableist, patriarchal, outdated, inflexible plans can be pitched as strategic even though the word "strategy" is generally used in a positive sense. Though I believed in moving money to those fighting for racial justice, I also believed we needed to use our voices, our reputations, and our collective power to speak up on behalf of Black people dying in the streets. For me, strategy included naming racism publicly as the culprit, especially in 2015, when so few philanthropic institutions were doing so. However, I didn't get to say this on our Zoom call. I was so taken aback my her response. Mary had written her script, asked for the conversation to be recorded, and said her piece.

Mary closed by saying:

> I understand more clearly that for you, our races (Black and white) created a real distance which I was not aware of, and I should have been, and I am partly to blame. I underrated the racial differences, perhaps in part, due to what I felt were positive open relationships I have had with Black women throughout my life, who they themselves were very much immersed in racial justice professionally and personally.

I do not doubt that Mary believed she was in positive open

relationships with Black women, but I think she might be surprised to find that some of those same women might agree, in part or in full, that they were *not* in a positive open relationship with her. Black women have very complicated relationships with white women, from the days when we had to share the same spaces with them in the big house, nursing their babies and avoiding their wrath, all the way through to the current workplace plantations.

When she finally stopped talking, I told her that I was surprised by her response, though I appreciated it. The extent of my surprise directly correlated with how progressive I perceived her to be. It seemed my stories had touched something deeper than I could even comprehend. I felt myself shrinking in response to her rebuttal but somehow managed to talk my way into this response: "I know I am not the only one negotiating relationships with white people across race and power. What I am hoping for here is to create a platform for Black women in this sector to see their stories and to know they are not the only ones." She parted with these words: "I am sorry you felt undercut and disrespected. I thought you should hear my perspective. I like to be honest."

* * *

THE IDEA for this book came about in 2019. Other funders were asking for documentation of our work and transformation. What did you do? How did you do it? How did you convince your board? We could have hired a consultant to interview the board and staff, and we could have produced a written report that would join the many sanitized reports published by philanthropic organizations year after year. I just didn't want to do it that way.

I wanted the telling of our story to have a raw quality. I wanted the reader to feel the pain of racism and understand what racism costs in terms of health and mental health. I wanted Black women to see their pain reflected in these pages. I wanted to document the inconsistencies that we struggle with both as people and as institutions. I didn't want the typical philanthropic success story. Though in many ways, this still is one.

if, A Foundation for Radical Possibility (formerly CHF) is a private foundation that challenged racism and classism by inviting Black people and people of the global majority with recent experience of homelessness, for example, to join the Board of Trustees and contribute to its vision, mission, and strategy. **if** then ceded decisionmaking power over its largest grantmaking portfolio to community members and built programs (like the guaranteed income pilot Let's GO DMV!) that center the lived experience of those who are struggling the most. This is a success in my book. The only failure is the rarity of these actions inside the philanthropic sector.

There have been efforts to challenge white supremacy in the sector, from *Putting Racism on the Table* locally to *The D5 Coalition* nationally. At the heart of the sector's stubbornness to change is a "near enemy" form of racism. In her book *Atlas of the Heart*, Brené Brown distinguishes the emotion *pity* from *compassion*. She says *pity* is a near enemy of *compassion*, while *cruelty* is its far enemy. She cites Texas researcher Kristin Neff, who writes, "'Near enemy' is a useful Buddhist concept referring to a state of mind that appears similar to the desired state—hence it is 'near'—but actually undermines it, which is why it's an enemy." Brown then goes on to say, "Near enemies are often greater threats than far enemies because they're more difficult to recognize" (2021, 119).

This sums up my feelings about the more progressive side of the philanthropic sector, where espoused ideas such as equity feel comparable to the ideas that many of us who come to the sector seeking liberation for our communities hold. Yet when we act on behalf of our communities, many white liberals (near enemies) seek to undermine us. They say we are not being strategic. They say we are too radical. They say we move too urgently. I spent so many years believing we were in it together. When I learned the truth, it broke my heart.

One could say I had been naive. Chris Rock asked in his Netflix special *Selective Outrage*, "How could Meghan Markle *not* know that the Royal Family, one of the inventors of colonialism, was racist?" Similarly, one could say I should have known what to expect in the philanthropic sector. I get it. No arguments here. I suppose I took for granted that I could bust through—dazzle them with my brilliance and poise, outpace them with my diligent efforts. Until I realized, after my health and mental health were in shambles, that white woman supremacy did not come to play.

---

1. Jessica's name has been changed because I was her employer at the time of this interaction.
2. This excerpt about Jessica did not make it into the final version of the book. You didn't miss it!

ACKNOWLEDGMENTS

I am always so moved by others' generosity and the gratitude that it begets, so I love writing and reading acknowledgments. I am so grateful for the many gifts of advice, encouragement, and critical questions I received in the nearly three-year process that it took to write this essay collection.

I want to first thank my writing coach, Mathina Calliope, who was teaching a class on memoir at Politics and Prose Bookstore when I decided to begin writing seriously. I wrote the essays "The Search" and "Tuskegee" in her class, and she stayed with me throughout the entire writing process. I also want to thank my main readers. Every month during the most intense months of writing, I sent them a batch of essays to review, and two weeks later, they sent back the most thoughtful comments and questions. Temi F. Bennett, Ronnie Galvin, and Hanh Le, you put in work!

Other readers who helped me with concepts, word choice, editing, section reviews, endings, and memory recall include Jennifer Beard, Whitney Benns, Tony Burns, Wendy Chun-Hoon, Tamara Copeland, Tamarre Daubon, Arline Geronimus, Alana Jones, Shauna Knox, Marshall Kreuter, Darakshan Raja, Silvia Salazar, Joan Sokolovsky, Aja Taylor, Lori Villarosa, Caroline Wang, Alan Weil, Lanita Whitehurst, Zenita Wickham Hurley, Nat Williams, Naima Wong, Terri Wright, Lisa Young, and David Zuckerman. Thank you for taking the time to offer helpful feedback that made each draft better than the last. Caroline, thank you for modeling the writing life!

When I was done with a clean first draft, I panicked about how this book would be received by white people, and a group of Black women sat me down over Zoom and reminded me that this was not about me. Even though they had not read the book, they wanted me to know that this was their book, too, and therefore I would not be alone. Maryam Abdul-Kareem, Tahira Christmon, BA Cockburn, Ruth LaToison Ifill, and Ricshawn Roane, thank you for that loving gesture. Thanks also to the countless other Black women who kept asking, "When is the book coming out?" You let me know that I had to keep going until the end.

I am indebted to my business attorney Domonique Price for her guidance throughout the writing process and the incredible Joyce Bond for the meticulous line editing of the entire collection. I also want to thank Raedorah Stewart for facilitating the writing of my book proposal. Susan Batten, I am grateful for your leadership in the sector. Thank you for your support of this work, including writing the book's foreword. I am also grateful to Safiy Sanchez for capturing a range of complex emotions on the book's cover; John Taylor for his work with Safiy on www.whitewomencry.com; and Jalisa Whitley, Nadia Frye Leinhos, Cindy Allman (bookofcinz), and Karen Vick for supporting me with the book launch.

To the Board of Trustees (current and former) and staff at **if**, A Foundation for Radical Possibility, thank you for trusting me with our story even though certain parts made you wince. I know it isn't easy to see our warts on the page. But one thing I have always appreciated is how you push yourselves into uncomfortable places to advance racial and other forms of justice. You don't shy away from the hard things, and sharing these experiences is hard. To my mom, sisters, and daughter, there were parts of this story that also included your pain. Thanks for being in life with me. We made it beyond the pain!

Finally, I can't close out these acknowledgments without loving on a few people. My friends know I don't do life without a circle of supporters. Thank you is insufficient for what my therapists and coaches have done for me over my life and career—Aviva Simonte, Andrea Holyfield, Sukari Pinnock, Marquessa Brown, Donna Alonso, Tosh Patterson, and Whitney Benns, you are beyond gifted. My mentor and friend David Harrington is no longer with us on the earthly plane, but I wanted to express my gratitude for his mentorship and leadership as the chair of the **if** board in 2019 and 2020. He was so proud that I was writing this book.

In addition to David H., I had no greater supporters than Temi F. Bennett and my partner, Ronnie Galvin. Temi and Ronnie believed in this book even more than I did at times. Temi, I will never forget your push to keep going. Ronnie, you are an anchor in the storm. Thanks for the many mornings, afternoons, and evenings turning over the complex issues I tackle in this book and wordsmithing with me as we typed in the same Google Doc. And your persistent question when I couldn't think of anything but the risks: "Is the risk worth it, Yanique? Only you can answer that." Thank you for holding space with me until I could say, "Yes, it is."

REFERENCES

Alexander, Michelle. 2010. *The New Jim Crow: Mass Incarceration in the Age of Colorblindness*. New York: New Press.

Allen, Mike. 2017. "Variables, Moderating Types." In *The SAGE Encyclopedia of Communication Research Methods*. Thousand Oaks, CA: SAGE Publications. https://methods.sagepub.com/reference/the-sage-encyclopedia-of-communication-research-methods/i15467.xml.

Badger, Emily, Claire Cain Miller, Adam Pearce, and Kevin Quealy. 2018. "Extensive Data Shows Punishing Reach of Racism for Black Boys." *New York Times*, March 19.

Baldwin, James. 1961. "'The Negro in American Culture': A Group Discussion (Baldwin, Hughes, Hansberry, Capouya, Kazin)." Recorded in 1961. Uploaded on January 17, 2016. YouTube video. https://www.youtube.com/watch?v=jNpitdJSXWY.

Barker, Jeff. 2015. "John Angelos Became Unexpected Voice in Freddie Gray Protests." *Baltimore Sun*, May 8.

brown, adrienne maree. 2010. "the return of the pleasure activist." *adrienne maree brown* (blog). November 11. http://adriennemareebrown.net/2010/11/11/the-return-of-the-pleasure-activist/.

———. 2017. *Emergent Strategy: Shaping Change, Changing Worlds*. Chico, CA: AK Press.

———. 2019. *Pleasure Activism: The Politics of Feeling Good*. Chico, CA: AK Press.

Brown, Brené. 2021. *Atlas of the Heart: Mapping Meaningful Connection and the Language of Human Experience*. New York: Random House

Brown, DeNeen L. 2013. "Julie Rogers to Step Down as Head of Meyer Foundation." *Washington Post*, June 11.

Diaminah, Sendolo, Scot Nakagawa, Sean Thomas-Breitfield, Rinku Sen, and Lori Villarosa. "How (Not) to Dismantle White Supremacy." The Forge, April 20, 2023. https://forgeorganizing.org/article/how-not-dismantle-white-supremacy

DiAngelo, Robin. 2020. *White Fragility: Why It's So Hard for White People to Talk about Racism*. Boston: Beacon Press.

Douglass, Frederick. 1857. "Frederick Douglass Declares There Is 'No Progress without Struggle.'" SHEC: Resources for Teachers. Accessed November 15, 2021. https://shec.ashp.cuny.edu/items/show/1245.

DuBois, W. E. B. 1903. *The Souls of Black Folk: Essays and Sketches*. Chicago: A. C. McClurg.

Fletcher, Michael. 2015. "What You Really Need to Know about Baltimore from a Reporter who has Lived There for 30 Years." *Washington Post*, April 28.

Fullilove, Mindy. 2004. *Root Shock: How Tearing Up City Neighborhoods Hurts America, and What We Can Do about It*. New York: Random House.

Geronimus, Arline. 2023. *Weathering: The Extraordinary Stress of Ordinary Life in an Unjust Society*. New York: Little Brown Spark.

Gibson, Cynthia, and Jen Bokoff. 2018. *Deciding Together: Shifting Power and Resources through Participatory Grantmaking*. GrantCraft. October 2. https://grantcraft.org/content/guides/deciding-together/.

Gray, Alysa. 2019. "The Bias of 'Professionalism' Standards." *Stanford Social Innovation Review*, June 4.

Hess, Kristen L., Xiaohong Hu, Amy Lansky, Jonathan Mermin, and Hildegard Irene Hall. 2017. "Lifetime Risk of a Diagnosis of HIV Infection in the United States." *Annals of Epidemiology* 27 (4): 238–43. https://doi.org/10.1016/j.annepidem.2017.02.003.

Hurston, Zora Neal. 2006. *Dust Tracks on a Road: A Memoir*. New York, NY: Harper Collins.

Ingraham, Christopher. 2014. "White People Are More Likely to Deal Drugs, but Black People Are More Likely to Get Arrested for It." *Washington Post*, September 30.

Kendi, Ibram X. 2016. *Stamped from the Beginning: The Definitive History of Racist Ideas in America*. New York: Nation Books.

———. 2019. *How to Be an Antiracist*. New York: Random House.

Kennedy-Moulton, K., Sarah Miller, Petra Persson, Maya Rossin-Slater, Laura Wherry, and Gloria Aldana. 2022. "Maternal and Infant Inequality: New Evidence from Linked Administrative Data." NBER Working Paper 30693. Cambridge, MA: National Bureau of Economic Research. http://www.nber.org/papers/w30693.

Leong, Nancy. 2013. "Racial Capitalism." *Harvard Law Review* 126 (8): 2151-2226.

LM Strategies. 2014. *The Exit Interview: Perceptions on Why Black Professionals Leave Grantmaking Institutions*. Association of Black Foundation Executives. https://www.abfe.org/wp-content/uploads/2014/05/ABFE-The-Exit-Interview.pdf.

Manson, Mark. 2016. *The Subtle Art of Not Giving a F*ck: A Counterintuitive Approach to Living a Good Life*. New York: HarperCollins.

Milk, Leslie. 2011. "Washington's 100 Most Powerful Women." *Washingtonian*, October 3.

Orfinger, Alex. 2013. "Why Julie Rogers Leaving the Meyer Foundation Matters." *Washington Business Journal*, June 12.

Politizane. 2012. "Wealth Inequality in America." November 20. YouTube video. https://www.youtube.com/watch?v=QPKKQnijnsM.

Robinson, Eugene. 2010. *Disintegration: The Splintering of Black America*. New York: Doubleday.

Rothstein, Richard. 2017. *The Color of Law: A Forgotten History of How our Government Segregated America*. New York: Liveright.

Sue, Derald Wing. 2015. *Race Talk and the Conspiracy of Silence: Understanding and Facilitating Difficult Dialogues on Race*. Hoboken, NJ: Wiley.

Thompson, Steve. 2022. "Lawyer: Investigation of Former D.C. Council Member Jack Evans has Ended." *Washington Post*, April 13.

Trent, Sydney. 2021. "A Racial Reckoning at Nonprofits: Black Women Demand Better Pay, Opportunities." *Washington Post*, July 11.

Verhaeghen, Paul, Shelley N. Aikman, and Ana E. Van Gulick. 2011. "Prime and Prejudice: Co-occurrence in the Culture as a Source of Automatic Stereotype Priming." *British Journal of Social Psychology* 50 (3): 501–18. https://doi.org/10.1348/014466610X524254.

Villanueva, Edgar. 2018. *Decolonizing Wealth: Indigenous Wisdom to Heal Divides and Restore Balance*. Oakland, CA: Berrett-Koehler Publishers.

Wardle, Tim, dir. 2018. *Three Identical Strangers*. CNN Films.

Wilkerson, Isabel. 2020. *Caste: The Origins of Our Discontents*. New York: Random House.

ABOUT THE AUTHOR

Dr. Yanique Redwood is an expert on racial equity and racial justice and has spent her career writing and speaking on these topics for nonprofit and philanthropic audiences. Dr. Redwood spent a decade as president and CEO of if, A Foundation for Radical Possibility, where she led the evolution of the foundation from a focus on health equity to a focus on racial justice. Dr. Redwood has degrees from Georgia Institute of Technology (BS) and University of Michigan School of Public Health (PhD, MPH). Her public health training is rooted in community-based participatory research approaches and an analysis of structural racism and compounding oppressions. In addition to her professional endeavors, she enjoys soca music, tending to her plants, skygazing, and reading with her book club Zora's Roundtable. She resides in Washington, DC and Montego Bay, Jamaica.

linkedin.com/in/dr-yanique-redwood

Printed in the USA
CPSIA information can be obtained
at www.ICGtesting.com
BVHW071020230823
668759BV00004B/14